LARRY WALSH

Cycling to Self-Discovery on the Southern Tier

SUIT
to SADDLE

Distribution by Bublish, Inc.
Published by Cabin Fever Press

ISBN: 978-1-647043-82-7 (Paperback)
ISBN: 978-1-647043-81-0 (eBook)

This is a true story. The author relied on extemporaneous notes, paper maps, data stored on a GPS device, videos, pictures, and memory in his attempt to accurately depict events as they occurred. All characters and organizations are real. All photos are the property of the author. *Suit to Saddle* is based on the author's view entirely.

To mom and dad.
Thanks for teaching us the true meaning of family.

"Dad, YOLO!"

Tara and Jaclyn on the beach in
Spring Lake, New Jersey
July 5, 2018

CONTENTS

FOREWORD

S uit to Saddle. That is certainly an appropriate name. However, "Headwinds" also works. That was a recurrent theme throughout the book and the "life journey" that Larry was on. He had been out of work for six months, struggling with the fact that his current vocation was not what he wanted upon his return to the workforce. Hearing him reveal that he wasn't sleeping, had been losing weight, and was experiencing anxiety all seemed like symptoms of depression. Exercise, which all five Walsh boys used as "stress relievers," did not help. Watching his son, Brian, play basketball—Larry's lifelong passion—seemed empty. But riding his bike around his hometown, Mendham, New Jersey, triggered something. He often imagined what it would be like to cycle from coast-to-coast on many cross-country business flights. The desire to test his limits, to reset, became a need.

He describes his cycling group as "everyday folks," but they were not—how many people do you know who have ridden cross-county unsupported? He repeatedly talks about the need to test his limits. As someone who completed Ranger training, those limits are expansive. Part of his motivation for cycling coast-to-coast was to forget about past challenges with which he had not coped well. His cheerful outlook and willingness to do the heavy lifting—carrying the heaviest group-gear bag—helped his group complete the ride together. His main contributions, a constant positive outlook and a spirit of cooperation, were what he could offer to their success.

He references riding into the winds in West Texas or the desert in California, how thinking of Kelley, Tara, Jaclyn, and Brian got him through the most challenging times. A long-distance runner myself, I appreciate that the mental challenges can be more considerable than the physical.

His desire to meet people—"take an interest, stop, listen, and people will amaze you"—and his catchphrase "Oh My God" expressing his excitement to ride his bicycle across the country reeled me in to keep turning pages.

We are a close family. Interwoven into his journey are repeated thoughts about his immediate and extended family. In the standard Irish fashion, the Walsh boys are stoic. Larry's feeling of low self-esteem was noticeable to us all, and even though we verbally gave him our support, he needed to figure out a way to regain his self-confidence and zest for life.

I enjoyed the reference to "pogey bait"—sweets and candy. He should have described our mother's grocery-shopping routine: five days a week to feed five growing boys, and the countless times when Mom bought 2.5 pounds of boiled ham and placed it in the fridge only to find Larry, within minutes, shove handfuls into his mouth. All Mom could say was "at least put it on some bread!!" I wondered about his barbershop fixation, thinking it must have been related to the "trauma" imposed by Dad when Larry and I were four and five, respectively, getting buzz cuts in the kitchen. It did save money!

It brought a smile to my face when he describes quickly falling asleep on the night before they left San Diego. Several of his brothers, myself included, would have been up all night, tossing and turning. Not Larry. He inherited that "gift" from Dad. He pays homage to our parents when he says "everything my parents did was for their children." Trying to emulate Mom and Dad motivates us all.

His personal and professional accomplishments are many. Division III college basketball player; Army Ranger; serving in Panama during Operation Just Cause; husband of Kelley; the father of two beautiful young women, Tara and Jaclyn, and son, Brian, who is ready to surpass all his sporting achievements.

Larry's close friends from his time in the military thirty years earlier, going out of their way to meet him in Austin, Texas. His pride in his service and reverence towards veterans. He often talks about the enjoyment of being a member of his local VFW post. I also agree that military service and athletic competition are two disciplines that bring out the best in people.

Visualizing Larry authoring a book was a significant stretch. But once I started reading his daily Facebook posts, which I did first thing every morning during his ride, his skill at this new endeavor was clear. His love for his country is plain to see, as is his respect for folks that do not have much, just Church and Family, and his desire to see people of all walks of life and backgrounds treated equally and with respect.

The rugged mountains in California or the over-100-degree heat in the Arizona desert. The sunset and sunrise at Usery Mountain, mosquitos in Louisiana and Mississippi. Meeting young adults from Brooklyn, Ukraine, and Russia on the road to Marfa, each beginning a new life, like Larry. He wrote about "peddling towards sunshine" the day he left El Paso, Texas. I believe he arrived.

Dr. Timothy Walsh
May 6, 2021
Mechanicsburg, Pennsylvania

INTRODUCTION

I retrieved my small nylon 1993 Oakland Athletics cinch sack carry-on from the upper bin when United Flight 1593 touched down in San Diego on September 15, 2018. I exited the airplane like I had hundreds of times before, except I was not wearing a business suit on this trip. The new green Columbia Silver Ridge™ convertible hiking pants I wore complemented my long-sleeve 10% spandex, 63% polyester, 27% nano bamboo charcoal ActivSkinz 100 SPF lightweight blue shirt and my new size 12 Salomon Contagrip outdoor shoes. I did not look to the signs that would direct me to baggage claim because I did not need to. Everything I needed for the next nine weeks was already in San Diego. I hailed a taxi and gave the driver the address for Bernie's Bike Shop on Cable Street. During the ten-minute drive from the airport to the shop, I thought to myself, "There is no turning back. I guess I'm doing this." I stepped out of the taxi in front of the bike shop after paying the fare.

It was a typical sunny Southern California early afternoon. The San Diego streets were bustling with shoppers and beachgoers. A few homeless people sat along the walkway. Seeing a combination of homeless people and beachgoers got me thinking, "Yes, I'm in California again."

I walked into Bernie's small, cluttered shop. Bikes were hanging from the ceiling and the walls and were crammed along the floor, everywhere, except for a narrow aisle leading to the cash register. At the register, I told the woman I was there to pick up the bike that I had shipped from New Jersey, courtesy of BikeFlights (a shipping service for cyclists). Roger, who ran the store, came out from the back room. He motioned me to come his way, and he led me to Tank, as I affectionately called my bike. It was rebuilt and looked to be in undamaged shape after the long journey across the country. Next to my bike were the four boxes I had also shipped. The boxes held my gear and all my belongings for the next three months.

I walked my bike out the front door, turned right, and then made another right into a side alley, leaning Tank up against the side of the building. I carried the four boxes out the side door and placed them on the ground next to my bike. Then I opened the four cardboard boxes, one by one. Slowly and methodically, I pulled out each piece of equipment and attached it to my bike. I connected the four panniers, two to the front rack and two to the back (a pannier is a bag designed to hold enough gear for self-contained rides over several days or weeks). I inserted five water bottles into separate bike bottle cages, two on the back of the saddle and three underneath and inside the triangle frame. I inspected every item I pulled from the boxes and meticulously placed each inside one of the panniers or attached it to the intended location on the bike. It was like putting a puzzle together, except this puzzle had a purpose: to transport me across the country. I paid Roger thirty dollars for assembling Tank and then took it, with the four panniers attached and fully loaded, for a short spin on Cable Street to ensure that everything functioned properly.

In the brief time I owned Tank, I had gotten a good feel for how it handled on the road. My keen sense of sound enabled me to detect vibrations or rubbing that required attention. I knew it well. Sure enough, the back tire was rubbing against the fender. The mechanic made minor adjustments, and then I was ready to go. I thanked Roger and waved goodbye. Before I pedaled away, Roger remarked, "A guy with one arm just left after picking up his bike." I gave him a nod, not thinking much of the comment. I was ready to start my journey.

I entered the address of the Marriott into my bike's GPS and began the short five-mile ride to the hotel. The glass doors automatically opened as I approached the entrance. I walked my fully loaded bike into the lobby and leaned it against the wall next to the front desk. I was assigned a first-floor room, so I did not have to drag Tank onto the elevator.

Upon entering the room, I unpacked everything that I had packed forty-five minutes before at the bike shop. It was essential that I figure out a packing scheme before the ride began. I separated the items into categories on the bed, table, chairs, side table, and on top of lamps. I tucked my clothing into the front right pannier. The rain and wintry weather gear went into the front left pannier. I placed my extra inner tubes, tires, tools, and water bottles in the right rear pannier; food and other miscellaneous pieces of equipment went into the left rear pannier. I attached my tent and sleeping bag to the rear rack behind the saddle. The waterproof paper maps, pocket light, pocketknife, dog horn, pen, waterproof pad, pogey bait, wallet, and personal identification fit into the front handlebar bag. I packed, unpacked, and repacked several times. If I practiced enough, I would remember where I'd put everything once the ride started. At least that is what I thought at the time. I wanted to be efficient.

My friend Clay and his wife Kristi were treating me to a steak dinner at the C Level Lounge on Harbor Island, overlooking the San Diego skyline. It was to be my last steak dinner until the night before I arrived at St. Augustine, Florida, nine weeks later. I had met Clay, a friend and professional colleague, in 1993. He was one of the few people I talked to about my idea to ride my bike from coast to coast.

Clay and Kristi pulled up in their car outside the Marriott. As I opened the car door and hopped into the back seat, I said, "Oh, my God, it's so great to see you guys! Can you believe it, I'm ready to go!" I reached forward and gave them each a big hug. "Clay, you know there's still time for you to change your mind and join me!" Clay smiled and laughed. But he had other plans. "I'm starting my new job after returning from vacation," he shared.

Over dinner, we talked about family and reminisced about life and unemployment. I had been out of work for six months and had previously confided in Clay about my lack of interest in returning to work any time soon. When they dropped me at the hotel after a two-hour entertaining and warmhearted dinner conversation, Clay and Kristi understood the road I had traveled getting to this point. Whether destiny explains the decisions I made, I'm not sure, but here I was, on the cusp of bringing to a conclusion months of drifting in contemplation. I was ready to go! "Good luck, so happy for you," Kristi said with genuineness of heart. Finally, after a long day of travel, I laid my head on the pillow and quickly fell asleep.

When I woke up the following morning, lifted my head off the pillow, and looked around the room, there was a nervous little feeling twirling around inside me. I realized I was one step closer to beginning my journey across the country. I wondered if I was out of my mind for taking on this challenge. I packed everything, walked my fully loaded bike through the lobby, and waved goodbye to the two front desk employees. The sliding glass doors opened, allowing me to walk my bike outside the hotel, where I gave a thumbs-up to the bell attendant. I entered the address for the San Diego Point Loma Hostel into my GPS and began pedaling away. The streets were quiet as I rode through neighborhoods on this warm and sunny Southern California day. As I approached the small red youth hostel on Udall Street, I found myself contemplating how I had gotten to this point, to this location, about to embark on a bike ride across the United States.

I was alone. I was anxious. I was about to meet ten strangers who had signed up for the journey just like me. Even before meeting anyone, I felt like a fish out of water. I had minimal long-distance cycling experience. (Twice when I was less than twenty years old I had ridden my bike over one hundred miles in a day, once with my younger brother Dan and a second time with a high school friend.) I knew tackling a cross-country ride was normally the pinnacle of a long touring career, not the first stride. I assumed the ten strangers I was about to meet would be experienced cyclists.

I hopped off my bike in front of the hostel. I looked up a narrow, short walkway that led to the front entrance. The bright California sun was shining, but I was protected from direct sunlight by two large palm trees that stood tall on the sidewalk. I leaned my bike against the outside wall, opened the door to the front entrance, and walked inside.

The front desk was empty. There was a bell and a sign that read "Ring bell for service," which I did. A young woman approached and welcomed me. I did not need to explain anything about my tour group. I was dressed in cycling shorts, a cycling shirt, gloves, and a sweat cap—my look gave it away. The woman directed me to the courtyard at the side of the building, where she said I could find others relaxing and hanging out. (This hostel was the starting point for all Adventure Cycling Association (ACA) Southern Tier Route tours.)

I walked outside to retrieve my bike and then headed for the courtyard. "Here we go!" I thought, apprehensive and excited at the same time. I had butterflies in my stomach. I opened the gate and saw a few people standing, one person sitting, and several bikes resting up against a wall to my right. A couple of people glanced in my direction but did not acknowledge my presence. I paused and looked around, wondering if these people were part of my tour group. I waved and said, "Hello!" to no one in particular. It was an awkward moment for me, as I had difficulty maneuvering my fully loaded bike through the narrow path leading to the communal area where others had assembled. I had not been this nervous since I delivered a two-minute oral debrief to over fifty soldiers from the 7th Infantry Division, including the commanding general and other higher-ranked officers, when I was deputized to represent my battalion, which deployed to Panama during Operation Just Cause in 1989.

I wondered if people were looking at me. I did not make eye contact to find out. The welcoming was a bit anticlimactic, as if what we were all about to tackle together was insignificant. "Hi guys, I'm Larry." I reached out to shake hands with a couple of other men. Wally, sporting a full greyish beard and displaying an air of confidence, was pleasant but unengaging, informing me he lived in Denver.

"I've spent a lot of time in Denver, but now I live in New Jersey," I offered, hoping to continue the conversation a little longer.

"I used to live in Morristown, New Jersey, and I know the good cycling roads in Morris County very well," Wally added, this time more interested in the exchange. I turned toward the other man, Tom, and asked where he was from. "I'm from Virginia Beach," Tom said, similarly pleasant but not interested in continuing the conversation. My first thought was that he looked like an experienced cyclist. He had a lean body and long, auburn hair that he wore in a high ponytail hanging over his shoulders.

My eyes focused on another man's calf muscles as I approached him to say hello. He had the face of a seventy-three-year-old man (which it turned out he was) but calf muscles reminiscent of an elite athlete.

I then introduced myself to Joel. It was a brief conversation; he shared that he was from the Seattle area, but not much else. I moved on to meet Travis, who was sitting at a picnic table toying with his bike tire. Travis was the most gregarious and engaging member of the group. He said, "I'm trying to figure what I should pack for the ride. I probably overpacked, but I still have time to figure it out!" I laughed. I understood his dilemma. Travis added that he hailed from San Francisco and had recently completed the ACA Tour Guide Leadership Course.

A woman walked into the courtyard from the hostel and sat next to Travis. I reached out to shake her hand. "Hi, you must be Joyce. I'm Larry. We talked a couple of weeks ago. I appreciated your advice. I decided to buy a Garmin and use the Ride with GPS app, not the Bicycle Route Navigator app." I had called Joyce, our tour leader, before arriving in San Diego, to ask for advice on which GPS device she found most useful for long-distance trips. It was another pleasant but unengaging greeting.

My first impression when I met Doug from Minnesota was that he was an outgoing person and an experienced cyclist. Within minutes of meeting Doug, I learned that he built bikes for a hobby and in 1976 was one of the original cyclists who rode across the country to christen the newly created TransAmerica Bicycle Trail in commemoration of America's bicentennial.

I also met Klaus, originally from Germany and visiting the United States for only the second time. He wore a colorful bandanna on his head and stood alone next to his bike in the back of the courtyard. He was a quiet man but, as we would learn throughout the journey, a man with many talents.

Deb and Gary from Chicago walked toward the back of the courtyard, looking for an open space to store their bikes. I initially hit it off with Gary, a six-foot-tall, two-hundred-pound man. "A Surly Disc Trucker, that's what I ride," Gary casually shared while introducing himself and his wife, Deb. "I had a problem with the back tire rim. After two thousand riding miles, the rim cracked. You might have the same problem too, because you're a big guy."

"That's good to know," I said. "The folks I bought the bike from in New Jersey told me I should be fine. I did upgrade from Continental to Schwalbe Marathon Plus tires," I added, as Gary and I continued conversing alone in the back of the courtyard.

We all gathered in the courtyard, getting to know one another. Everyone was low key, engaging in light conversation, filling up uncomfortable silence with small talk. We set up our sleeping arrangements for the two-night stay at the hostel before beginning the trek east. I was assigned to a room that had two bunk beds and a single bed. I grabbed one of the lower beds, and Joel took the other lower bed. Doug grabbed the single, and Klaus chose the top bed above Joe. No one chose the top bed on my side.

We all went about our business, settling into our rooms, making small talk, but mostly getting comfortable in what would be our home for the next two nights. I brought the four panniers with all my equipment into the room for safeguarding. Why I thought I needed to safeguard my equipment, I do not know. My greatest fear initially was whether I would fit in. But after meeting everyone, a heavy load was lifted from my shoulders—partly because I had finally met my new family, the ones I would share my life with for the next nine weeks, twenty-four hours a day, seven days a week. I was also reassured when I saw that everyone was of average size and built just like me. All except one were retired. Only one person sported the enormous cycling thighs and calves reminiscent of Tour de France elite athletes. They were all everyday folks, like me.

On this night, two nights before we left on our long journey, we sat around a fire in the middle of the courtyard, reintroduced ourselves, and shared our motivation for riding the 3,100-mile Southern Tier route. There were ten cyclists from the United States and one from Germany. Dan, hailing from Southern California, joined the group just before everyone grabbed a chair to get comfortable around the fire pit. The flickering light and random crackling sounds supplied the perfect environment for the aura of anticipation that filled the air. Joyce opened: "Welcome to San Diego and the Adventure Cycling Southern Tier ride." One by one, we all shared our motivation for being there. I was uneasy about how much to disclose about my journey to San Diego. My wife, Kelley, my eldest brother, Tim, and my sister-in-law, Gina, knew the details. No one else did.

Whether to share the details had remained a dilemma for me, until now.

When it was my turn, I told them I had often imagined what it would be like to cycle across the country. On many coast-to-coast business trips, I would look out the airplane window and marvel at the landscape below. Flying from Los Angeles to Newark, New Jersey, leaving the hustle and bustle of city life, I had found myself lost in wonderment as I gazed at the snowcapped mountains. I imagined what it was like to live in a small community surrounded by a vast wilderness. I thought about the westward migration. I was in awe at the enormity of our great country. I fiddled with my hands, wondering what would come out of my mouth next. I told the group that I was between jobs and had decided to take advantage of the time off to meet the challenge. I looked forward to riding through the California desert, testing my limits, meeting new people, and experiencing something I had thought was only a pipe dream. At fifty-six years of age, I wanted to dive in now rather than wait to fulfill this bucket-list goal after retirement. All of it was true, but there was more that I was not ready to reveal.

Before calling it a night, we divided up the group gear. This ride was self-contained, meaning you carried everything on your bike, with no support vehicles. Everyone would carry their own equipment plus one item of the group gear. I sat quietly, waiting for my turn to choose an item. I was the last to select and was stuck with the bag of utensils. It was the heaviest and most cumbersome of all the items, so of course no one chose it. It was now mine to carry.

I was the least experienced cyclist in the group, by a long shot. Doug, Tom, and Wally had previously completed the 4,200-mile TransAmerica Bike Route from Virginia to Oregon. Dan was on round two of crossing the country on the Southern Tier route. Joel had crossed the country, from Washington to New Jersey, once before. Travis, Deb, Gary, Klaus, and Joyce were also on their maiden cross-country voyage, but each had racked up many miles in the saddle touring lengthy distances. While I knew little about long-distance cycling, I knew my legs were strong and ready for the challenge.

Wally asked if I was okay with carrying the bag of utensils. I expressed my concern that I was unsure if I could keep up with the group, therefore arriving at camp later than the utensils would be needed to prepare dinner. Wally told me not to worry, that I would be fine. I wanted to be a good team player, so I gladly accepted the challenge. I felt like I had passed the first "new guy hazing" phase. I was excited and anxious but ready for what was next.

When I was healthy, my usual exercise routine had included playing basketball with the guys. But on December 17, 2017, I tore the plantar ligament in my right foot. On this fateful day, when I fell to the ground in pain, I realized my basketball playing days would be suspended for a long time. I was frustrated, angry, and demoralized. Since I had turned fifty, every year, on cue, I injured my calf muscle, usually in the middle or toward the end of a game. Suddenly I would hear a pop, and down I would go. Three months later, I would return to the court, only to have the same injury repeat itself again and again. But this injury, the torn plantar ligament, was more severe. I knew it right away.

Playing with the guys on my over-fifty basketball team was a favorite pastime, besides spending time with my family. For a bunch of older guys, we played very competitively. Everyone had a love for the game. We would compete to win. After a win, we would gather in the bar next to the gym to watch NFL football and talk smack. After a loss? The same routine, but the conversation focused on how poorly we'd played and the adjustments needed for the next game. The camaraderie was incredible.

Shortly after injuring my foot, I lost my job at a pharmaceutical company. It was March 5, 2018, and it started out as a typical Monday morning. I arrived at the office ready to begin the day. I glanced at my iPhone to check email before entering the building and saw that the CCO had scheduled a meeting with me. I walked into my boss Mike's office, and I could tell right away something was up. His usual expressive, pleasant leadership style had given way to an uneasy, detached demeanor. He was giving off a bad vibe. He knew something I did not, and he did not want to tell me.

"Brent wants to see me. Do you know anything about the meeting?" I asked Mike.

Mike seemed fidgety. He raised his head, looked in my direction without making eye contact, and with a resigned sigh told me, "Larry, go have your meeting with Brent." I turned around, left his office, and walked to my cubicle. It was 9:00 a.m. I had an hour to contemplate my meeting with the CCO.

The week before, Kelley and I, along with my boss and his daughter, had hosted the 2017 top sales performers at the annual President's Club award trip to the Cayman Islands, compliments of my employer. The night before we visited Stingray City, the company president shared an update about the company's reorganization that he had announced several months before. Hearing this message, I realized my job was in jeopardy. I had always expected the company to reassign me into a different role or business. But for some reason, on the way to Stingray City, I had a bad feeling in the pit of my stomach. Legend says you will get seven years of good luck if you kiss a stingray on its head. It couldn't hurt, so that is what I did.

I had returned from my trip relaxed and invigorated. I had kissed that stingray and was hoping for the best.

The news of a company downsizing hits affected employees like a ton of bricks. By the end of the day on Monday, March 5, all employees, including those who kept their jobs, learned the fate of dozens of us who did not. Even though only the senior leadership team knew what was going on, there was an ominous feeling in the air. I sensed that this Monday would be my last. I had an uneasy feeling as I knocked on Brent's door. The meeting with him and a human resources representative was brief and professional. I walked into the office, sat down next to the HR representative and across from the CCO. Then unfolded the start of an uncomfortable conversation: "As you know, the company initiated a Project Accelerate organizational review several months ago. As a result of that review, your position has been eliminated . . . Megan will now review your severance and benefits," Brent said in a matter-of-fact manner.

After Megan reviewed my benefits, she asked, "Do you have any questions?" Everyone stopped talking when I looked up at Brent and said my parting words. "It's difficult to receive this news. And I appreciate how difficult it is to deliver it. I'll be fine. My only anxiety is calling my wife to tell her I lost my job." I walked back to my cubicle, paperwork in hand. I sat at my desk, alone, trying to process what had just happened. I texted Kelley, "Kissing the Stingray didn't help." She responded with the prayer emoji. I gathered up my belongings, took my employee ID from my belt, and placed it on top of my desk. Shortly after that, I walked out of the building for the very last time. Eleven years of working for this company had come to an end, just like that.

I thought I was prepared for what lay ahead. However, with no job and not getting any exercise because of my torn ligament, I began a downward spiral.

A few weeks later, Kelley and I and our son, Brian, took a trip to St. Petersburg, Florida, to visit Kelley's family for spring break. What should have been an enjoyable trip turned out to be the most challenging week of my life. I felt out of it. I walked aimlessly along Gulf Boulevard in St. Petersburg, waiting for Kelley's relatives to arrive. When they did come, I was physically present—mingling with family on the beach, at the pool, at the outside grill—but disconnected emotionally from everything. Feelings of inadequacy consumed my thoughts. I was not sleeping. I was not eating. Nothing I took part in was pleasurable. I knew I needed help when I watched my son play basketball with his cousin and I did not want to be there. Kelley convinced me to go for a jog one morning. I forced myself to jog a couple of miles, hoping to break a sweat and disrupt the vicious cycle. My inability to sweat when the heat index rose due to the combination of sun, elevated temperature, and high relative humidity buttressed my belief that I needed professional help.

I realized I was suffering from depression. The sense of despair I felt was real. Objectively, I knew things were not that bad. My marriage was excellent, and my kids were amazing. Financially, we were okay. I simply could not move beyond my feeling of helplessness. Kelley called my older brother Tim, a physician, and told him what I was going through. The night before we returned home from Florida, I received a call from my brother. Tim opened with, "I talked to Kelley." I jumped right in and said, "I don't know, Tim, for some reason, I can't break it. It just hit me pretty fast." I continued, "I found a counselor and a psychiatrist back home. I have an appointment with each first thing Monday morning. I'll call you after." I could sense his concern for my well-being and his desire to help. I told him I was not sleeping well, was embarrassed, and had lost my self-esteem.

Tim and I had similar conversations eleven years before when I was first diagnosed with depression. In 2007, I lost my job with Pfizer Pharmaceuticals, a company I had dedicated many years to and loved working at—so much so that I picked up and moved my family five times, twice across the country. The loss of that job hit me hard. I remembered that the feeling I had in 2007 was like what I was experiencing this time. I felt like my mind was in a prison cell, surrounded by walls. I was not able to think or see anything except darkness. My mind raced as I tried to break the vicious cycle. Nothing helped. I tried walking a couple of times, thinking I would receive help from a little exercise. On one afternoon in April 2018, a few weeks after I had lost my job for the second time, I ran into a friend in Morristown, New Jersey. He looked at me and said, "You've lost a lot of weight." I pulled it together and made up an excuse, but I knew I did not look well either.

I was afraid, embarrassed, and ashamed of myself. I felt like a child as I told Kelley that I needed her by my side. I did not want to leave the house. I felt vulnerable. I was a shadow of myself. I had been a six-foot-four, 230-pound former college athlete and Army ranger, and that person was gone. Kelley and my brother Tim were my foundation. Without their support, concern, and love, I am unsure where I would have ended up.

My psychiatrist was trying to figure out the best combination of medication to help with my sleep, mood, energy, and interest in life. Once a week, I drove to the medical building for my appointment. I parked the car and tried to avoid seeing anyone when I walked up the stairs to the doctor's second-floor office entrance. Infrequently, when I saw someone entering the medical building, I looked away to avoid making eye contact.

I had found this psychiatrist when I was in Florida. I did not have a referral; he just happened to be the first who would accept my medical insurance and could see me the week I returned to New Jersey. At our first meeting, I broke down before getting two words out of my mouth. I regained enough composure to share the details of my situation. For years, when I was a sales representative for Pfizer Pharmaceuticals, I sold medications that treated depression, anxiety, and other mental health disorders. It was an odd feeling sitting alone in that room waiting to be invited in to see a shrink. This was not supposed to happen to me. But it was.

I was taking my medication, looking for a job, and still not feeling great when New Jersey had a bad snowstorm in the middle of March 2018. The storm dropped heavy wet snow, resulting in tree limbs breaking all over our property. I mustered enough energy to clean up around our home, hauling heavy branches to the front of the house, which eventually would be picked up by the town. This physical activity helped focus my attention on a specific goal, that of cleaning my property. When the weather started to improve toward the end of April, I began riding my bicycle around my hometown of Mendham, primarily for exercise.

Finally, after seven weeks, I went from being miserable and concerned about my mental well-being to waking up every day with vigor, energy, and a sense of purpose. I started to appreciate the time off from work. Slowly I began dreaming about the future and what I wanted to do. Depression no longer confined my thoughts to the emptiness of a prison cell. I was sleeping better, and my outlook on life improved.

I felt like I had a purpose when I woke up in the morning. I wanted to get out of bed and begin the day. I did not know what to do, but I knew I wanted to do something. I thought about a friend and former work colleague who had walked the Appalachian Trail (Georgia to Maine) the year before and posted daily updates. I had been hooked and could not wait to read his daily summary. I remembered thinking how cool that experience was and how I wanted a challenge like that. My thoughts about riding my bike across the country came back to me. I was, and still am, a dreamer, and I have always had a habit of acting on my dreams.

When I was a twenty-two-year-old, graduating from college, I was the only student out of 398 to receive a commission through the college Reserve Officer Training Corps (ROTC) and enter active military service (a handful of other students received commissions as reserve duty officers). I strived to be different. When most soldiers followed a well-defined military career path, I chose the road less traveled. My plans were unorthodox. My dreams were *my* dreams. I requested to be reassigned to Korea for a hardship tour after two years at Fort Polk, Louisiana, serving as a 2nd lieutenant in the 1-55 Air Defense Artillery Battalion of the 5th Mechanized Infantry Division. (Tours in the United States are for four years. According to the Department of Defense, soldiers serve hardship tours in locations where the quality of living is significantly lower than in the Continental United States. Soldiers receive an extra stipend referred to as hardship duty pay).[1] While serving in Uijeongbu, the Republic of Korea, in Camp Stanley just north of Seoul (location of the 1970 film *MASH* and the CBS television series *M*A*S*H* and site of the 4077th Mobile Army Surgical Hospital), I volunteered and got accepted into the Infantry Officer Advanced Course and Ranger School, usually reserved for career infantry officers. I saw scrawny guys proudly wearing the ranger tab, and I figured if they could complete that course, then so could I. I wanted to put myself in demanding situations and challenge myself to new limits. What could be a more bracing and significant challenge than riding a bicycle across the country?

I was glad I followed my gut and did not go back to work. The layoff from my job was a blessing in disguise that I did not realize at the time. Now, here I was in San Diego with my new "family," ready to begin my trek across the country.

---

1   Militarybenefits.info

Chapter 1

CALIFORNIA
(BLUE SKY, RUGGED MOUNTAINS, AND DESERT)

September 17 – San Diego–Shakedown Ride (3 miles)

I n the days leading up to the ride, there were many moments when I asked myself, "Am I really going to doing this?" But here I was, really doing it.

It became very real during my shakedown ride along the Ocean Beach Bike Path on September 17, 2018. (A shakedown ride assesses the bike to uncover problems that should be resolved before departing on a long bike ride.) We arrived at the edge of the path and walked our bicycles through the sand to the ocean for the ceremonial dipping-of-the-tire-in-the-Pacific-Ocean ritual to christen the start of the journey. A handful of people were walking on the sand close to the surf, some with dogs and others alone. It was a quiet, balmy morning. By a little after 8:00 a.m., the temperature had climbed to over eighty degrees, but ocean air was chilly. Blue skies hovered over us, and wispy clouds covered the distant sky. Eleven cyclists were smiling, snapping pictures, and soaking up the moment. We looked at each other and beamed. Far in the distance to the south, I saw the Ocean Beach Pier jutting out from Niagara Avenue, which connected to the street leading to downtown San Diego. Closer to our location, a rock jetty served as an excellent backdrop for some of the pictures that would highlight the start of our day. Everyone was relaxed, absorbing the moment, a moment I had thought about for a long time. Dipping my bike tire in the Pacific Ocean would become one of many milestones forever etched in my mind.

September 18 – San Diego to Alpine (43 miles)

We woke up at five thirty and began preparing to leave San Diego. We ate breakfast, packed, and secured our gear onto our bicycles. Tank, my new grey Chromoly steel-framed Surly Disc Trucker touring bike, equipped with four fully loaded panniers, fully loaded front and back racks, front handlebar bag, bike pump, and five water bottle cages, was ready to go. The handlebar resembled an airplane cockpit control panel, with everything I needed to navigate directly in front of me, including an iPhone 8, a Garmin Edge 1030 GPS device, an additional Garmin battery pack, a dog horn, a rearview mirror, a gear shifter, and brakes. As we walked our bikes single file through the back section of the hostel to the street, a sense of calmness entered my mind. You could hear a pin drop. I could not believe it. I was about to ride my bike across the country. The next time I saw my family would be after fulfilling this momentous goal.

The first half-mile riding east on the Ocean Beach Bike Path was eerily quiet. The serene Pacific Ocean sounds and tranquil views slowly diminished, replaced by the sight of concrete and buildings and the distinct sounds of car and truck engines whistling by as we approached Interstate 5 above the bike path. We eventually met San Diego rush hour traffic on this Tuesday morning. My primary navigation tool was the Garmin 1030 (a last-minute purchase). I carried two backup navigation tools: ACA waterproof paper maps and an iPhone 8 with the Southern Tier route loaded on the Ride with GPS app.

Several of us made a wrong turn before exiting San Diego city limits. We backtracked about a mile to find the correct route. About ten miles outside of San Diego, my group gear nearly fell off my front rack. Luckily for me, I was stopped at a red light when I noticed the bag of utensils hanging loosely unsecured next to my front tire. I reattached and made sure it was correctly fastened before continuing. Figuring out how to pack using bungee cords to keep things secure was a challenge. It was sweltering, over ninety degrees, the sun beating down, zero breeze, and the hills were giant. It was not a wonderful way to start my journey!

My quest to become a long-distance touring cyclist began on June 22, 2018. I remember the day well. It hit me on the way home from a fifteen-mile bike ride in my hometown of Mendham, New Jersey. I walked into the kitchen area where my wife was standing, and her friend Nancy was sitting on a bar stool at the counter. I told my wife I was considering a cross-country ride. In hindsight, I said "considering," but my mind was already made up. I was serious about riding coast to coast.

Kelley knew I needed to take this on. She was one hundred percent behind me. Nancy encouraged me as well. I began searching online for cross-country bike routes. I also started to watch YouTube videos to learn how to cycle long distances. The more videos I watched, the more excited I became. The stars aligned when I found a self-contained cross-country bike ride organized by the ACA that began in San Diego on September 15, 2018, and ended in St. Augustine, Florida, on November 20, 2018.

I called the ACA tour department. A woman named Emma answered the phone. I explained that I was a novice cyclist and asked whether my age (fifty-six) and lack of experience should deter me. She calmly quelled my concerns, saying that most people who ride coast to coast on the ACA tours are of retirement age. First impressions are so important. I honestly do not know if I would have taken the next step, the decisive action, if not for Emma's can-do attitude and positive energy.

I needed to buy an excellent touring bike and camping equipment, such as a tent, sleeping bag, air mattress, cycling clothing, safety equipment, and other essential items. Emma suggested a couple of different bike brands, one of which was Surly. (I owned a Fuji road bike, which was not designed to withstand the rigors of a long-distance bike ride.) I was not fully committed just yet, but I knew decision day hung in the balance.

I raised the umbrella to shield us from the sun and looked at my wife and kids; this was the day I was making my decision. Spring Lake Beach at the Jersey Shore buzzed with activity on this July 4th holiday week. "I want to ask your opinion," I said to my kids. "I've been thinking about riding my bike across the country and wanted to know what you guys think about that idea." Without hesitation, my girls were all in. Tara, twenty-six, and Jaclyn, twenty-two (at the time), shared their sage advice: "Dad, YOLO!"

"What does that mean?" I asked.

"You only live once!" they said with a smile.

That was the clincher. I made the decision. Or so I thought.

There were plenty of times when I had second thoughts. I often questioned whether I was making the responsible decision. I had zero income and a family to support. Saving money for retirement and my children's college education were our family's financial priorities. I agonized over it for days. I could not think of anything else but the bike ride.

Things became clearer when I thought about the Christmas season. I imagined sitting in the same chair I had spent many hours in, contemplating my future and being disappointed in myself for not taking this fantastic opportunity to follow my dream. If I did not take the plunge, I knew I would regret not going for the rest of my life. I had told just enough family and friends about the trip to hold myself accountable. I did not want to back out. I knew I was ready to go, but I had no idea of the extent of the commitment I was about to make.

I rode my bike around Mendham, thinking about the pros and cons. On one shoulder was my angel, telling me to go for it. On the other, my brain, telling me to be responsible and get a job. On the saddle of a bike, along the country roads of Morris County, New Jersey, I found myself thinking about life, my family, and riding through the California desert.

The day I finally made my decision, I chose to stay off the saddle. Before I committed, I wanted to make sure I could muster the same enthusiasm for the journey when I was off the saddle. Sure enough, as I sat in my home office watching a YouTube video of someone who had ridden through the desert on the Southern Tier, it hit me.

"I'm doing this!" I shouted. Kelley heard me scream and walked into my office.

"What is going on?" Kelley asked.

I shouted again, "I'm doing this!"

I paid the $4,900 fee to the ACA. I ordered a new Surly Disc Trucker from Whippany Cycle in New Jersey. Chet, the cycle shop owner, supplied priceless counsel to me as I considered different equipment options. I made about a dozen trips to REI to buy essential equipment. I evaluated various cycling gear during training rides, often returning items I did not need. Overpacking is one of the biggest mistakes novice long-distance cyclists make, and despite my best efforts, I did too.

Leading up to the ride, I watched many cycling videos, learning as much as possible in the abbreviated time I had to prepare. I taught myself the ins and outs of long-distance cycling. What to pack? What to wear? How to prevent back and knee pain? What are the most challenging aspects of the ride? Another question I asked myself: what if I blow a tire? The last time I remembered changing a bike tire was in the late 1970s and early 1980s when I rode to Ocean City, Maryland, from my hometown of Camp Hill, Pennsylvania. I took short videos on my iPhone of the mechanics at Whippany Cycle changing a tire and fixing a broken spoke or chain, in case I needed to repair my bicycle in the middle of the desert. For the next several weeks, I trained daily to prepare myself for what lay ahead. My training routine consisted of cycling about thirty miles per day twice a week with a fully loaded bike (weighing more than eighty pounds). In addition, I rode the stationary bike in my basement and lifted weights three days every week. I entered the Ramapo Rally on Sunday, August 19, and rode the sixty-five-mile leg in the annual New Jersey bike rally.

At the rally, I met a cyclist who had recently completed the TransAmerica Bike Tour led by the ACA. I listened intently as he talked about his experience. He recommended upgrading from the standard Surly Continental tires to Schwalbe Marathon Plus tires. He also highly recommended navigating using a Garmin GPS device. The Monday after the rally, I ordered a new Garmin device and Schwalbe tires. I was one hundred percent focused on preparing myself for the ride in the weeks leading up to my departure. I became obsessed with completing the Southern Tier bike ride.

During this preparation time, I was also looking for a new job. But deep down, I knew I did not want to go back to work yet. I contacted a few friends who were networking on my behalf. I told them my professional goals had not changed, just my timing. I told them I would reconnect and continue my job search when I returned to New Jersey in December. A couple of friends gave me hope that I would have job opportunities waiting for me upon my return. I needed to believe that so I could focus my efforts on the ride. For the three months I rode the Southern Tier, I kept an extremely positive attitude, which helped me navigate the tough times on the road.

Just as I had thought, I was one of the last in the group, lagging. I felt okay but struggled to find a rhythm. About twenty miles east of San Diego, I entered Mission Trails Regional Park on the Father Junipero Serra Trail. The bustling San Diego scene was now behind me. Turning into the park, I soaked up the clear blue sky, the surrounding mountains, and the slight haze. I felt as if I was leaving one dimension and entering another as I departed the hustle and bustle of San Diego and pedaled into the often-hiked wilderness surrounding the popular Cowles Mountain.

Just a few weeks earlier, I had been experiencing sorrow and sadness. Now here I was incredibly appreciative that somehow I'd made it to this point.

One of my fellow cyclists had difficulty climbing the hills leading out of San Diego. I stayed with him to make sure he was okay. We would cycle a couple of miles and then stop to rest. We repeated this pattern for several miles. At the crest of one of the most challenging climbs, I stopped at the Casino Inn Bar & Grill on Alpine Boulevard, a neighborhood watering hole in east San Diego County, to rest, rehydrate, and refuel. Stopping at cafes, bars, and convenience stores became routine over the next nine weeks.

Dan, Doug, Tom, Travis, and I initially rode to the wrong campground about four miles off-route. It was late afternoon, sunny and hot, the end of a long day. Exhausted and unable to contact others in the group, we were frustrated, not knowing where to go. It took us about an hour to figure out where we'd made the wrong turn, but we eventually arrived at the proper destination, the Alpine campsite.

The first full day on the saddle was now behind us. We had ridden forty-three miles and climbed 3,500 feet. My body felt surprisingly good, and Tank had performed like a charm. The campsite was tranquil. The trees supplied much-needed shade, allowing us to escape the ninety-degree temperature and the sun that beat down all day. We ate dinner and gathered around the picnic table to discuss the next day's ride. Pasta, bread, salad, and a pastry dessert were on the menu.

Cooking and cleaning duty rotated. It reminded me of kitchen patrol (KP) duty when I was in the military. It was not my night to cook, but I helped clean the pots and pans. I put leftover food in the park bathroom to secure it from critters. The sun still peeked through the eucalyptus trees but was going down quickly. We all used our headlamps to conduct our map meeting, which would become a nightly ritual. During map meetings, the entire group gets together for thirty minutes to review the route, available services, weather conditions, and accommodations for the following day and night.

My friend Jeff came to mind. In 2017 he had captured details of his hike on the Appalachian Trail with daily posts. I imagined other friends of mine were feeling the same way about my ride that I had felt when following Jeff's hike the year before. I wanted to share my experience in a way that gave others a sense that they were riding with me. I settled into my Big Agnes tent and wrote my first of many daily Facebook posts. I had not been on Facebook prior to this ride, but I was persuaded to open an account by my wife and kids. I wrote from the heart and did not overthink anything. For about five minutes on most nights, tonight being the first, I shared stories, feelings, observations, and pictures. I called Kelley. "Hi, it was a fairly good day. I am tired but feeling okay. We're staying at the Alpine campground tonight. I'm starting to get a lot of Facebook friend requests. Love you, I'm calling it a night." With that, I closed out day one on the saddle.

September 19 – Alpine to Jacumba Hot Springs (44 miles)

I woke up rested, feeling good, ready to go, and prepared for the day ahead. I took down my tent, packed my gear, and loaded Tank. Steam was rising into the morning air from a large pot of water on a small camp stove. The first order of business every morning: coffee! It was a must. The rotating cook, usually the first to wake up, lit two backpacking stoves. One was to prepare hot water for coffee and oatmeal. The second pot of hot water was combined with chlorine tablets to clean utensils at the end of each meal. For breakfast, we normally ate cereal, oatmeal, breakfast bars, yogurt, and fruit. We made sandwiches for the road for lunch, and some of us carried "pogey bait" (sweets and candy). After breakfast, I performed ABC morning preventive maintenance checks (Tire Air Pressure, Brakes, Tighten Bolts, and Clean Drivetrain) and then hopped on the saddle. Generally, it took ninety minutes from the time I woke up until departure.

The whole group started riding each morning between seven and eight-thirty. We wanted to ride many miles before the temperature rose. On this day, day two, the temperature hit 106 degrees. The sun beat down all day. Riding the California hills east of San Diego was particularly challenging. Thankfully, there were very few cars on the road.

We began riding through small towns. I stopped at a little convenience store in Pine Valley, California (population 1,500). I reapplied sunscreen and filled eight water bottles (five attached to my bike, two inside my right rear pannier, and one attached by a bungee cord to the rear bike rack) and my CamelBak hydration pack.

About twenty miles west of Jacumba Hot Springs, our destination for the night, I stopped at a vantage point on Old Highway 80 and State Route 94 in clear view of the wall separating Mexico from the United States near the Baja California Peninsula. I had read about and listened to the constant back-and-forth between both sides on the topic. Do we build the wall, or don't we? People were passionate about the issue. The loudest voices launched invective attacks, and news had become so toxic. I did not know what to believe. I wanted to see the wall up close, educate myself, and form my own opinion.

State Route 94 leading to Jacumba was narrow, one lane each way. Downtown Jacumba Hot Springs offers little more than the Jacumba Hot Springs Resort and Spa, our lodging for the night. I imagined riding up to a magnificent resort entrance where we would be met by an employee who would pamper the group during our short stay. The opposite happened. It took me a few minutes after entering Jacumba to find the resort. The nondescript brown stucco building and small gravel parking lot blended in with barren farmland and a few dilapidated buildings surrounding the area.

A car filling up at a gas station and a handful of parked cars in the gravel lot were the only signs Jacumba was not a ghost town. It was too early in the journey for me to completely grasp what a unique experience it was for me to ride through small rural communities in the western part of the country.

Dan led the pack for the first few days. He generally arrived at camp two hours before I did. When I arrived at the Jacumba Resort, Dan was swimming in the pool, enjoying time off the saddle. I wondered if Dan's strategy would remain the same all the way to Florida, if he would lead the way and set the pace each day. There was no time limit, no rules, and we did not have to ride together. Everyone naturally rode at a different pace, depending on skill level, strength, personal motivation, and desire. Some rode in pairs. Others met up at a rendezvous point to eat lunch, but everyone arrived at the destination before dinner was served, typically between five-thirty and six. I rode on my own and at my own pace 90 percent of the time. That way, I could take pictures, talk to the locals, take it all in. I focused on one day at a time, thinking about the next milestone and completing each ten-mile segment.

I drew the lucky straw—no roommate in Jacumba—which meant I did not have to contend with snoring. There were typically two to a room each night we stayed at a motel, to keep costs down. The $4,900 fee covered food (except pogey bait) and lodging expenses (campsites, churches, motels). The rotating daily cook carried the group credit card to buy food and handle the organization of food delivery to the next destination. It was hard to feed eleven hungry souls with a $125 daily budget, but we managed. Shopping at Dollar General and Walmart, which we often did, increased our purchasing power with the small stipend distributed for each day.

After settling into my motel room, I left the group and walked across the street about a quarter mile further south to see the wall up close. The brown desert-floor path that led me to the wall was full of tumbleweeds. To my left, I saw a baseball field overgrown with weeds. On my right were several ranch homes, little more than shanties, lining the path leading to the wall. I did not see a lot of human activity. A couple of children and adults were outside one home in front of a large rusted pickup truck. A desolate wilderness surrounded me. About fifty yards from the wall, I entered an area that was fenced off, but I did not think I was trespassing. "Well, here I am," I said aloud, but to one in particular. I reached out and touched the wall. I saw brown mountains and a few tiny houses nestled in the hills about one hundred yards from the border on the Mexican side.

The newer section of the wall was about fifteen or twenty feet high. The older section was much lower and needed an extreme makeover.

The older part appeared to me to be made from leftover scrap metal. I wondered if the project was underfunded, so people used their creativity to complete the task. The older area appeared easy to mount, but the newer section would be challenging to scale. A small metal sign attached to a ten-foot-tall metal pole sticking up from the brown desert floor communicated vital information, an unmistakable message for the intended audience to heed government advice: "Warning—International Border—Unlawful to enter except at ports of entry!" The sign struck me as necessary but not practical. I assumed many people trying to enter the United States in Jacumba Hot Springs were doing so because they did not want to enter at the ports of entry. Plus, the nearest ports were in Tecate and Calexico, forty miles from Jacumba.

I am struck by the negligible impact that seeing and touching the border wall had on changing my perspective. To me, it is simple, not complicated, and does not have to be so political—just like vetting who can enter the White House, which is a good idea. The same logic applies to entering the United States.

The group of eleven were getting to know each other, starting to form personal connections. The faster cyclists hung together. The folks who had previously completed cross-country rides and already understood what to expect led the way. I was one of four on their virgin journey. I was still trying to figure things out, not wanting to overdo anything until I was comfortable knowing what to expect riding a significant number of miles on consecutive days. Back at the resort, I called Kelley, let her know I was doing well, had survived day two, and was on my way to finding my groove.

September 20 – Jacumba Hot Springs to Brawley (57 miles)

This day started with anticipation—I would finally ride through the California desert! I once saw a picture of a cyclist riding alone in the Imperial Sand Dunes, the sun beating down, nothing in view as far as the eye could see. This picture was etched in my mind. I envisioned swapping places with that person.

I was chasing a dream. However, I still had questions that I hoped this bike trip would help to answer. Was this ride an attempt to fill a void in my life? Was this ride my answer to regaining my self-confidence? Or maybe I just like adventures. In any case, I was about to enter the desert on a bike! I was excited beyond belief.

We started the day riding on Interstate 8. It was my first time riding on an interstate. I had an adrenaline rush before descending through Devils Canyon and the In-Ko-Pah Gorge on a seven-mile, 6 percent grade down to the desert floor. I paused and looked out over the vast landscape. I could see the blue sky in the distance protruding above the eye-level cloud cover. There was no wind at the top of the mountain. However, I expected to meet wind gusts as I picked up speed and descended, twisting back and forth through switchbacks to the valley below. I was on top of the world, looking down into the canyons. I saw jagged mountains. Directly to my right, on the ground, lay a lonely mattress. It appeared that someone had dumped it there or that it fell off the back of a passing vehicle. It was incongruent with the picturesque landscape before me. Looking at that mattress, I had a sinking feeling something would fall off my bike and cause me to crash, making me unable to continue. The mattress sighting was peculiar, completely unexpected, and out of place. I took a deep breath and started the descent.

I applied brakes for the next twenty minutes, never exceeding thirty-eight miles per hour. It took time for me to adjust to riding a bike that weighed close to ninety pounds. I did not know if the panniers would remain attached to the racks at such high speeds. I was completely focused on the task at hand, my mind locked in on speed and safety. I wanted to accelerate and let my adrenaline take over, but I also did not want to die. If I tumbled over, the result would not be good for me or my bike.

"I made it safely," I thought, as I slowed down at the bottom of the mountain. I wondered if Doug, about thirty minutes ahead of me, had exceeded fifty miles per hour, a speed he'd exceeded on prior cycling tours.

Cycling on the interstate in the western part of the country is not uncommon. I could not imagine riding on the shoulder of Interstate 80, 287, or 95 in New Jersey. That would not be safe. I experienced less traffic and found the road shoulders much broader on western interstate highways. After completing the descent, weaving in and out of the canyons, I saw an exit for Calexico. About one quarter mile further, I saw a large sign for the Yuha Desert (part of the Sonoran Desert).

I stopped to take in my surroundings. I thought about the poor souls who rode the Southern Tier route east to west. Climbing the mountain we had just descended would be extremely challenging. Windmills by the dozen dotted the desert floor. I was curious about how much electricity the windmills produced.

To the north, I saw the Coyote Mountain range. It was difficult to estimate distance—so much vastness. What appeared to be a couple of miles away was actually ten or fifteen miles, if not more. I thought about rain causing flash floods, overwhelming the desert wadis (dry channels that can fill up and flood an area without warning during the rainy season).

Cloud cover filled the sky. Rain was not in the forecast, but desert weather can be very unpredictable. I thought about what actions I would take if a flash flood threatened the area. In the distance, looking east, I saw a bridge over a wadi. As I approached, I realized the bridge was under construction. With all the technological advances, I could not believe my GPS device had not informed me about the bridge construction! I had a destination to get to—obstacle or no obstacle, I had to find a way around. I was stuck on Evan Hewes Highway with the Coyote Mountains to the north and the Yuha Desert to the south, an impassable bridge in front, and a wadi underneath me. In the distance, the skies looked threatening. The wispy clouds turned into menacing rain clouds the further east I gazed.

Three other group members, Travis, Deb, and Gary, arrived at the bridge minutes after I did. I surveyed the situation, assessed that the construction zone was only thirty to forty feet long, and decided the best course of action was to continue through the bridge rather than underneath. So that is what we did. Shortly after crossing, I received a text from my hometown friend Gino, who was following me on the Garmin tracker app. He asked where I was. I told him I was in the middle of the California desert, surrounded by wilderness, riding on a road that seemed to go on forever!

Gino and his wife Angela hosted a small gathering of friends in Mendham the night before I left for San Diego. They, along with my family and a few friends, were interested in my journey. I had agreed to send updates as much as I could. I did not know if I could get into a routine of posting frequent updates on my ride. Being active on social media is not typical behavior for me. However, it did not take me long to pivot. I made a point of sharing my thoughts most every night before bed. My nightly Facebook posts became my way of staying connected with family and friends, closing a daily chapter, and preparing myself mentally for the next day's adventure.

The worst stretch of pavement during the 3,100-mile trip was on the Evan Hewes Highway. The pavement surface on this extended stretch of road left something to be desired. The road was torn up, and pebbles were kicked up as I rode. I could not help but think that if I were Evan Hewes, I would demand that my name be removed and not associated with the road. There was a rumble strip every ten feet for the twelve-mile stretch between Calexico and El Centro, California. The vibration and audible rumbling were transmitted through the bike and up my body. I was concerned about my tires blowing, spokes breaking, screws loosening, and even a rack falling off. I worried about whether these types of roads would be the norm for the rest of the trip to Florida. I hoped not.

From the construction zone to El Centro, I rode with the youngest member of our group, Travis. He rode with a BOB (beast of burden) trailer connected to his bike. Travis was one of two in the group who carried their gear in a BOB. All others rode with panniers. In my view, riding with a BOB has one main benefit: unpacking and packing is easier because there is only one place to put gear, rather than four. I suppose there is some logic to that way of thinking. But if I did it again, I would still ride with panniers.

It was essential to stay hydrated, especially in the desert where resources were scarce and there was a snowball's chance in hell of finding a potable water supply. Heat exhaustion was a concern for everyone. Shortly after leaving the construction zone, Travis told me he was down to his last bit of drinking water. I gave him one of the extra water bottles I kept stashed away in a pannier. At the time, several more miles remained before we entered El Centro. I was happy to help.

El Centro looked like a speck in the distance at first, but as I got closer, I could make out the built-up area's urban footprint, surrounded by vast open land. El Centro is the largest city in the Imperial Valley and the county seat of Imperial County, California, a sprawling area. Growing industries including retail, professional services, health care, leisure, and hospitality are adding jobs to the primary agricultural sector.[2]

Even though I generously applied sunscreen every day, my arms and legs had become darker than I could ever remember. Dust and dirt coated my suntanned skin. My lips were chapped and blistered from the sun and wind. I became sun blind when I took my sunglasses off to wipe sweat from my eyes, and I dealt with temporarily impaired vision while adapting from dim light to sunlight. My five-hundred-dollar Oakley prescription sunglasses were a godsend, ranking as one of the essential items in my possession. I placed my iPhone inside my handlebar bag because the temperature was too hot for it to remain exposed to sunlight. The hot sun beating down unfiltered directly on the paved dark black asphalt road made for a truly memorable desert cycling experience and an alternate way to obtain the perfect suntan without using reflective tanning blankets.

After I refilled my water supply at a convenience store at the intersection of Main Street and Old Highway 111 in El Centro, I rode

---

2   www.cityofelcentro.org

north for the last twenty miles to the Gateway Church in Brawley, our destination for the night. The ride was nerve-racking due to the narrow shoulders. Numerous trucks passed, and a lot of debris (small pieces of wood, tiny pieces of metal) littered the road. I was thankful when I arrived safely at the church after a stressful twenty-mile ride through the Imperial Valley, ever mindful of the large volume of rush hour traffic speeding in both directions. I stocked up on drinks and pogey bait at a Walmart across the street from the church. The group talked about the next day's ride at our map meeting, which was expected to be the most challenging to date. I was excited, anticipating the passage through the Imperial Sand Dunes, a day I had looked forward to since I first began researching this trip. There was a good chance the only store between Brawley and Palo Verde, our destination, was closed, which caused anxiety for some group members, including me. We expected the temperature to reach 106 degrees again the next day.

The group decided to get an early start to rack up miles before the heat pounded down on top of us. Sprawled out on the floor of the church's social room, I put in my earplugs, an essential piece of equipment, and fell asleep. I strategically placed my air mattress and sleeping bag on the opposite side of the room from the loudest snorers. Two cyclists snored as loud as Adam Sandler did in the 2000 *Little Nicky* movie when he falls asleep on the rocks overlooking a city. It was much easier to create separation when sleeping outside at a campground. Inside a confined area, noise is magnified tenfold, while outside, the noise dissipates, so the snoring is much more tolerable.

September 21 – Brawley to Palo Verde (71 miles)

We were up and ready to go at six-thirty the next morning. I had been looking forward to this day for a long, long time. As I approached the sand dunes from the west, I could see the landscape change in front of me. The lush green agricultural farmland gave way to pure white sand for as far as the eye could see. I stopped when I saw the warning sign, "Possible drifting sand next seven miles, drive with caution."

The Imperial Dunes reminded me of the white sand of Panama City Beach, Florida, and that of the White Sands National Park in New Mexico, on the list of the world's greatest natural wonders.[3] I had visited these two places years before. Now, I felt like I'd landed on Mars, with the mountains of white sand on all sides and one pedal rotation away from entering a different civilization. The barren area, where little rain falls annually and dunes reach heights of three hundred feet above the desert floor, is a sought-after destination for all-terrain vehicle riding enthusiasts.[4] I flashed back to the picture of the cyclist riding in the Imperial Sand Dunes and realized I had fulfilled a dream. I was content and satisfied. But I also started to run low on water. I saw a sign for a ranger station and rode up a small hill about a quarter mile off-route to search for water.

Hope turned to distress when I realized the station was closed. I opened the door to the men's bathroom and glanced at a bare room with a single squat toilet toward the back. I drank the little water I had left in one of my water bottles. I then resorted to drinking the remnants of water that had spilled into the bottom of the right rear pannier. I was nervous, not knowing if the Glamis Beach Store, about twenty miles further east, was open.

Doug led the way when we left the church in Brawley. This was Doug's second cross- country bike ride. His first was in 1976, when he joined the first group to ride the famous TransAmerica Bicycle Trail from Yorktown, Virginia, to Astoria, Oregon. Here he was, forty years later, in retirement after a long and successful career as a mechanical engineer, riding coast to coast a second time. He sent everyone a text message: "Glamis store is open!" It was great news and the single best text message

---

3   nps.gov

4   www.blm.gov/visit/imperial-sand-dunes

I received the entire trip. I was so relieved when I saw that message. It was 105 degrees, and I was out of water when the text came through.

We all took a break in the shade at the Glamis store. Gary and his wife Deb, exhausted from the brutal riding conditions, hitched a ride in the cab of a pickup truck for the remaining forty miles to the Palo Verde campground. Due to the never-ending road vibration on the Evan Hewes Highway, Gary's rear bike rack screws had come loose, resulting in one of his panniers being compromised. Shortly after leaving the Glamis store, Joel fell off his bike after experiencing heat exhaustion. Another Good Samaritan transported Joel and his bike to the campsite in Palo Verde in the back of his pickup truck.

Fifteen miles east of Glamis, Klaus, Travis, and I met border patrol agents at a border station on State Route 78, smack-dab in the middle of the Midway and Chocolate Mountain ranges. The border agents were all very agreeable, but they meant business. They did not allow me to take a picture with them in it. We told them about our struggles since leaving San Diego, especially the difficulty of riding in such extreme heat. One of the agents shared a story of another agent who had recently tracked down drug smugglers in the surrounding hills, an undertaking that was complicated by the extreme heat and unforgiving rugged hiking conditions. After speaking with the agents, we sat in the shade underneath a sizeable portable tent away from the direct sun and watched them perform their duties. Cars and trucks stopped at the checkpoint. A dog circled the vehicles, searching and sniffing. A border agent placed a device underneath each vehicle to detect illicit drugs. Each encounter lasted two or three minutes.

Klaus, from Germany, decided he could not continue cycling to the campsite in Palo Verde, for safety reasons. He told us he was not accustomed to riding in such extreme heat. Klaus cycled without shoe cleats and rode with very thick bike tires. This combination had given rise to the challenges he faced, causing him to have to work harder than he should have, especially in those brutal riding conditions—not ideal equipment for such a long tour. The patrol agent asked someone driving a truck with a cab if he would transport Klaus to the campsite. A Vietnam veteran graciously agreed to help. He was on his way to watch his grandson play a high school football game in Palo Verde on this day, Friday, September 21.

Everyone eventually arrived safely at the campsite in Palo Verde after a difficult day on the saddle. Our host, the campsite manager, made lasagna for dinner and served cherry pie for dessert. Both were exceptionally good and hit the spot. I slept on the ground that was cushioned with soft sandy soil, and the canopy of palo verde trees supplied much-needed shade. During the map meeting, a discussion ensued about the challenges we endured riding in such extreme heat. A few expressed frustrations about the riding conditions; three members, Gary, Deb, and Klaus, did not feel safe continuing. They planned to rent a van and drive to El Paso, Texas, at which point they would join the group to continue the journey to Florida. We supported their decision, wished them well, and hoped to see them again.

The enthusiasm, positive energy, and heartfelt stories we all shared at the nightly map meetings about people we met and places we saw started to wane. I began to sense friction between individual members of the group. Some projected their insecurities onto others, consciously or not, taking out their frustrations. I started to hear people complain about food choices and sleeping accommodations, and little whispers pitting one against another. I did not pick up any significant issues, just apparent annoyances expressed by some. I made a mental note but kept my focus on the big picture: St. Augustine, Florida.

I knew there would be challenges along the way. Many would be out of our control. But what *was* in our power was how we reacted to each challenge. When things got tough, my positive attitude and cooperation were my best contribution to the team—carrying the heavy and bulky bag of utensils highlighted and revealed my desire to be a team player. What I lacked in long-distance cycling knowledge and experience I made up for in my willingness to carry a heavier load. However, only four days after leaving San Diego we were dealing with team conflict. I wanted to set a positive example of how to deal with adversity. I listened to and acknowledged the concerns expressed. I shared my hope that we would see each other again in El Paso and then refocused the team back to the next day's ride. There was nothing we could do about the weather. How we responded to it was a different story. That was my focus. As it turned out, the ride from Brawley to Palo Verde would be the last time the entire eleven-person group rode together.

Doug, Deb, and Gary mentioned that the ride to Palo Verde was one of the most difficult they had ever endured. I thought it was tough, too, for sure, but it was also an enjoyable day on the saddle. I was sleeping well, and this night would be no different. I called Kelley and shared the highlights of my day with her. Typically, our conversations lasted about ten minutes. I always asked how the kids were doing. She shared any updates. My son Brian's eighth-grade football season was underway. My eldest daughter, Tara, out of college for four years, worked at Boston University. And my middle daughter, Jaclyn, a recent college graduate, had started working. I was content being on the road, away from home. I knew my wife had everything under control.

Chapter 2

HELLO, ARIZONA!
(DESERT, DESOLATION, AND DEBRIS)

September 22 – Palo Verde to Quartzsite (44 miles)

O ur morning departure was bittersweet. We said a hearty farewell to the three riders who left the group. The rest of us continued our trek with the anticipation of crossing the Arizona border. My first Starbucks stop of the trip was in the town of Blythe, California. I leaned my bike against a table outside the store. Like at any other Starbucks experience, people were sitting down, chatting, and drinking coffee. I sat with Travis, who was resting and drinking coffee as well. Fifteen minutes passed, and I decided to hit the road again. Recharged after finishing my tall regular coffee, I started riding again, not wanting to get too comfortable. We still had many miles ahead of us, and the temperature would exceed one hundred degrees once again.

Shortly after I left Blythe, I crossed the Colorado River and entered Arizona. I could see a large white Arizona border sign ahead. A sense of fulfillment overcame me as I approached. I thought, "Wow, I just rode my bike across the state of California! How cool is that!" One state down. Only seven more to go. Crossing each state border was an important milestone. Gratitude flowed through me as I paused to think about the journey. I sent a picture of my bike next to the Arizona border sign to my wife, kids, parents, and four brothers. I received encouraging responses, including a few thumbs-up emojis.

My body had held up well through the first few days. But today, my fingertips on both hands started to go numb. Both of my feet also started to bother me, becoming very painful with each pedal rotation. The constant pedaling and pressure on specific nerves caused my extremities to lose feeling. My younger brother Dan, a radiologist and an avid cyclist, recommended that I move my hands continually to lessen the numbness. I followed his advice. Moving my hands and feet helped for a few miles. However, within minutes after pedaling again, the numbness returned, and so did the foot pain. I took several short rest breaks to regain the feeling in my hands and feet. Sometimes my feet became so painful I just looked up to the sky and yelled, "Stop!"

I still have numbness in all my fingertips and, oddly, the middle toe on my right foot. My hands are very stiff every morning. It takes me a minute of rubbing and moving my fingers around before I can use them for any productive activity. My knees rarely bothered me. My lower back did not cause a single problem, and except for a few hundred miles riding through Texas when saddle sores caused discomfort, the adequate rest, excellent equipment, proper riding posture, and my overall fitness level contributed to sustained good health.

Before leaving for San Diego, I read about a condition known as Shermer's neck. According to an article on the website PubMed, ultra-distance cyclists are most susceptible to the condition, when neck muscles fail from fatigue after several days on the bike and can no longer support the head.[5] I became very aware of the slightest neck soreness, which I

---

5   Berglund B, Berglund L. Shermer's neck is a rare injury in long-distance cycling races. Association with diplopia described for the first time. Lakartidningen.

got occasionally, but fortunately, that was it. In the back of my mind, I wondered whether I would fall victim to Shermer's neck. It can happen abruptly to anyone.

However, the bigger problem for me was that my lower legs and hands started to swell. I had learned about kidney function when working for Pfizer Pharmaceuticals selling medicines that treat heart disease. Fluid was beginning to accumulate in my extremities. When I touched my legs, they felt like rocks. The feeling is like that of muscle swelling when fluids flow to muscles to repair the "damage" after a challenging workout. But my leg swelling was due to my kidneys not releasing waste naturally through urination.

Doug, Tom, and I had been riding at the same pace on this day. Shortly after entering Arizona and Interstate 10, we exited the interstate at a truck stop. The excessive heat and challenging hills had taken a toll on us. I struggled to reach the truck stop exit along Interstate 10, climbing through the Dome Rock Mountains, a foreshadowing of the weeks ahead.

I drank a lot of water and rested until the leg swelling went down. It eventually subsided after about an hour of sitting and resting out of the direct sunlight. I was not going to quit. I hopped back on my bike and continued riding along the shoulder of Interstate 10. Tom had continued riding about thirty minutes before I departed the truck stop. The conditions were so extreme that Doug decided to hitch a ride on the back of a pickup truck to Quartzsite, Arizona, our destination for the night. (Strangely, this was the only time on the entire trip when my legs swelled to the point that I stopped and dealt with the problem.)

I became concerned about my health at this point. I wondered if my age was a factor. I thought the heat was slowly eating away at my insides, and that I would suddenly pass out from dehydration. Blisters had formed on my nose and ears due to direct sunlight for several hours a day.

2015 Dec 15; 112:DR71. Swedish. PMID: 26671432. PubMed,

I repeatedly dodged road debris. Road shoulders were full of shredded 18-wheeler truck tires, rubber, nails, you name it. There was no shade. The beating sun and the extreme heat had me thinking for the first time that completing this journey would be an extraordinary achievement.

The first time I rode on an interstate in California was exhilarating. Going fast, descending through twisting, winding roads on Interstate 8 down to the desert floor, a sense of freedom and acceptance that I was doing something cool, overwhelmed me. But now, the novelty had worn off. I no longer wanted to ride on the interstate. About ten miles further east, after leaving the truck stop, I exited Interstate 10. I made a beeline for an overpass that was about five hundred yards in front of me to my left. I leaned my bike against the large circular concrete support beam underneath the overpass. I sat down on the angled, rough concrete ground and struggled to get comfortable. My body slid down due to the slant, but at least I was sheltered from the direct sunlight. It was a welcome break before completing the last seven miles to Quartzsite, Arizona.

The official ACA Southern Tier Tour includes fifty-seven riding days and ten rest days. Each day we rode a finite distance, averaging between forty and eighty miles. I set my GPS to ping every ten miles. It was easier for me to focus on completing ten-mile segments than completing a 3,100-mile journey. Every ten miles achieved was ten miles closer to St. Augustine. Repeat, repeat, repeat until the finish. That is how I thought about it.

My mind often wandered. Anything to help pass the time. I thought about my childhood in a small ranch house in Wantagh, Long Island, where my family lived until 1971. I thought about my dad teaching me how to play baseball when I was a little kid. I thought about our family attending St. Frances de Chantal Roman Catholic Church on Jerusalem Avenue in Wantagh every Sunday and every Holy Day of Obligation. When all five boys behaved in church, Mom and Dad treated us to Dunkin' Donuts or Carvel Ice Cream. I had great memories of visiting my grandparents in New Bedford, Massachusetts, fishing in

Clarks Cove, and playing basketball with my brothers and cousins at E.R. Hathaway Elementary School in New Bedford, where my aunt was principal. When I was in fifth grade, I started playing basketball and football after our family moved to Pennsylvania. I dreamt about playing in the NBA. I did not initially want to go to college. I thought I would become an electrician if I could not make the NBA. But then reality hit me. I attended college and joined the Army ROTC program. After my seven-year active-duty Army service, I married Kelley, started a family, and began my professional career in the pharmaceutical industry. The time on the road allowed me to retrace my tracks and reflect on decisions that shaped the person I am today.

Quartzsite, the rock capital of the world,[6] is a small western community surrounded by rocks, sand, mountains, and the vast open Sonoran Desert. The small town (population 3,677) about 130 miles west of Phoenix is a mecca for RV camping, attracting people from all over the country. Every year in late March, thousands attend a weekend camping and music festival called the Rock Fiesta. There was not much happening in town when I was there.

After we settled into our rooms at Hi Jolly's Outpost on Main Street in downtown Quartzsite, we walked about a quarter mile to Dairy Queen for ice cream. My ability to influence the group took center stage. I convinced them that ice cream would taste great after a day of cycling through the Arizona desert. Honestly, it did not take much convincing. The foremost benefit of riding a bicycle long-distance is that you can eat anything, anytime, anywhere, and still lose weight. Cycling coast to coast is the single best weight reduction program, period! I give my guarantee every person will lose at least twenty pounds. The catch is, it is a three-month program, and there are no shortcuts.

---

6   Quartzsitetourism.com

September 23 – Quartzsite to Harcuvar (37 miles)

Between seven and ten in the morning is the most enjoyable time to ride. The chilly, still air and rising sun form the perfect environment to think, relax, and reflect. Winds pick up around 10:00 a.m., and then the combination of extreme heat and constant rolling hills brings about strenuous riding conditions. I had previously read about the four dreaded, horrible H's: humidity, heat, hills, and headwinds. When all four are combined, they form another H: hell! So far, we had only dealt with two H's, hills and heat. But on this day, the most trying of the four horrible H's, headwind, reared its ugly head and took center stage. I would rather ride in temperatures over one hundred degrees or climb a steep 15 percent grade than deal with headwinds. Even slight headwinds are challenging to ride through. The moment I stopped pedaling, my forward momentum ended. There is no coasting into a headwind. Numerous times, I looked toward the sky and yelled, "Stop! Enough already!"

I reflected on my time in California. We had dealt with mountains, hills, and heat. It was incredibly challenging to be on the saddle, but exhilarating nonetheless. Arizona turned out to be a disappointment for one main reason. The roads were smooth, but weaving back and forth often to avoid retread, or "road gators," and tiny pieces of steel strewn along the road's shoulder from shredded truck tires wreaked havoc on my psyche. The tiny pieces of steel, referred to as "steelies," caused more flat tires than anything else by far. Arizona's barren bone-dry desert wilderness consisting of cactus, sagebrush, sand, rocks, and mountains is a world unto itself.

I regularly performed preventive maintenance checks and services (PMCS) on my bike. One of the many lessons drilled into me when serving in the US Army was that PMCS were performed before, during, and after any military equipment use. Performing PMCS reduces the chance of a mechanical problem occurring while the equipment is in use. If I inadvertently rode over debris, I stopped to check if steel had penetrated my tires. I paid close attention, making sure to avoid potholes or uneven pavement, to prevent bike damage. At a convenience store on my way to Harcuvar, Arizona, the destination for the night, I pulled a piece of steel out of my back tire. The steel was tiny, but shiny, making it easy to see. The combination of paying attention, riding with excellent tires, and performing routine PMCS all contributed to a smooth start to my cross-country trek.

Dan stopped at the same place I did to rest and refuel his body. I thought back to when I arrived in San Diego and hailed a taxi to Bernie's Bike Shop. Right before I pedaled away after retrieving Tank, the store manager casually mentioned that a guy with one arm had recently picked up his bike. During our first group orientation at the hostel, I met Dan, the guy with one arm. At age sixty-five, he was embarking upon his second cross-country bike ride. He had competed in several Iron Man competitions and had a full arsenal of one-arm jokes. When he introduced himself to the group, he said he felt a need to "prove himself." In unison, we all chimed in, "Dan, you have nothing to prove!" Dan is a fantastic person. He injured himself as a young man in an industrial accident and was lucky to be alive and lives every day with that mindset. Dan carried a full pack, just like the rest of us. After our rest break, I took a short video of him leaving the convenience store. He looked at me and smiled as he rode by. That ten-second video is one of my favorite memories.

On the way to Harcuvar, I passed by the towns of Hope and Morristown, a Mexican restaurant, a sign advertising a place to fix flat tires, and a sign pointing in the direction of Happy Valley Road. A simple sign comes to life when nothing else is around. I thought of my friend Bill Clinton (a college basketball teammate) and the place called Hope, and Morristown, New Jersey, a short distance from my hometown. And I could not imagine any other place in the United States called Happy Valley other than Happy Valley, Pennsylvania, home of Penn State football. Many of the buildings I rode by in between small towns were dilapidated or abandoned. Roads leading nowhere were commonplace; clues of a better past were visible here and there.

For the first week on the road, I escaped the real world. I did not watch television. But on this night, I watched about fifteen minutes of NFL football in the recreation room at our KOA campsite in Harcuvar. It was a good change of pace to watch a little TV. Before settling in for the night, I received a phone call from my older brother Tim. He informed me that my dad had a health problem and had gone to the doctor for a checkup. I went to sleep feeling concerned, not knowing the details about my dad's health. My brother said my dad did not want him to share the news with me. I was glad he did. Before leaving in the morning, I spoke to my sister-in-law, Gina, who shared that Dad was fine. I was relieved, thankful, and ready to hit the road again.

Through their actions, my parents raised us the right way. The family was and still is a priority. Our parents taught us to judge actions, nothing else. We were instructed that good people come from all walks of life. That mentality holds true today. I did not realize it at the time, but everything my parents did was for their children. The bonds that were formed remain strong. We all look forward to family get-togethers. We poke fun at each other, talk about our kids, and enjoy each other's company. I wake up every day wanting to be the best parent I can be. I learned from the best.

Joel was our resident weatherman. He was also the oldest member of the group. At seventy-three, Joel was riding his second coast-to-coast ride—his first self-contained, unsupported ride. Ten years earlier, after retiring from the railroad business, he had ridden his bike, supported, from Seattle, Washington, to Avon-by-the Sea, New Jersey, in thirty-three days! His wife carried his gear in a vehicle. Each morning before leaving, Joel planned how far he would ride that day. His wife would go to a motel in the town or city and wait for Joel to arrive. They repeated this for thirty-three days until arriving at the Jersey Shore.

Before beginning his railroad career, Joel served in Vietnam as an Army dog handler. One night, he showed the group a picture of himself and his dog companion leading a patrol in the Vietnam jungle surrounded by a squad of soldiers. Joel and I formed an unspoken bond, having both served. We talked about our military experience two or three times; that was it.

Joel always knew the forecast and wind direction. I usually did not pay attention to his weather reports. My feeling was that I would not do anything different. I was riding regardless of the weather conditions. If it started raining, I would make the call on the spot whether to don rain gear. Plus, ninety percent of the time, the forecast was wrong anyway. On this night, Joel did warn us that rain was in the forecast for the first time since we left San Diego.

September 24 – Harcuvar to Wickenburg (59 miles)

About an hour after departing Harcuvar, I rode into the famed Maricopa County, which for months headlined national news due to Sheriff Joe Arpaio's immigration policy. The idea of Sheriff Arpaio passing me on US Highway 60 in a vintage 1950s Dukes of Hazzard Plymouth sheriff patrol car on a high-speed chase after ne'er-do-wells popped into my head.

Feathery, fluffy, white clouds high above transitioned to darker, sinister, low-hanging clouds as I got closer to the town of Aguila. The vistas of an infinite landscape gave way to sagebrush, tumbleweeds, and a lot of cactus, the clouds obstructing my view more than on any other day since departing San Diego the week before. I felt isolated, riding solo through small rural communities: Salome (population 1,530), Wenden (population 728), and Aguila (population 798). In one moment of comic relief shortly before I entered Wickenburg, a single cactus plant caught my attention because it appeared to be giving me the finger. The massive column protruded from the ground, with several branches extending from the main stem. One of the arms pointed forward while the others remained erect. Think three fingers down and one finger raised. It made me laugh.

We were making substantial progress, knocking out forty to seventy miles per day since leaving San Diego. One day at a time, and eventually we would make it to Tempe, Arizona, the endpoint for section one of the ACA Southern Tier Route. (The Southern Tier consists of seven sections.) But first, we enjoyed a night camping under the stars at the humorously named Horspitality RV Park (I love the cacography) in Wickenburg. Wickenburg is a small rural town in Maricopa County, discovered in 1863 during the gold rush. Today it is known as the dude ranch capital of the world and the team roping capital of the world.[7] There was a lot going on for a community of six thousand people. At our map meeting, we talked about our ride to Tempe in the morning. We all looked forward to relaxing on a well-deserved rest day. Self-contained cycling tours sponsored by the ACA typically include a rest day for every seven to ten days on the saddle. Time off the saddle is essential to help the body recover, plus it allows riders to run errands and visit the sights.

My Big Agnes tent was an ideal purchase for this ride. During my first shopping visit to REI before leaving New Jersey, I explained to a sales associate that I wanted to purchase high-quality and lightweight equipment to take on a cross-country bicycle ride. She recommended the Copper Spur HV UL2 Big Agnes Tent (2 lbs. 13 oz.), an extra-long REI co-op insulated air pad (1 lb. 4 oz.), a three-season REI co-op sleeping bag (3 lbs. 2 oz.), and Sea to Summit waterproof cycling bags. I added two colorful shirts (blue and yellow), three pairs of dark cycling shorts, and a bright red Showers Pass inclement weather jacket to my shopping cart, for a total cost between $1,500 and $2,000. The Big Agnes is easy to carry and easy to set up. There is plenty of room for my tall frame, and it is durable. The potential for rain was low in Wickenburg, but still, I used the tent rain cover for the first time. We all woke up to dry ground—another false weather report.

---

7   ci.wickenburg.az.us

September 25 – Wickenburg to Tempe (74 miles)

It was another scorcher of a day when we began our ride through the Vulture Mountains and rode over the Central Arizona Project canal into the valley below, approaching Surprise, Arizona, the westernmost area of Phoenix proper. I envisioned exiting the mountains through switchbacks and looking out in the distance at a new civilization. What came to mind was Joseph Smith and his Latter Day Saints followers in the mid-1800s. I pictured them on their pilgrimage from upstate New York to Salt Lake City, Utah, looking down through the mountains east of Salt Lake City. I visualized an incredible reveal as I looked out to the vast wilderness coming out of the high desert. I was amped up. I was anticipating an experience like downhill snow skiing in the tuck position, intensely focused on avoiding any missteps that could ruin my day, finally making it to the bottom, exhaling, and thinking how cool that experience was. But, before I knew it, I was riding along a straight flat road approaching the outskirts of Phoenix. The romantic experience I had hoped for was not meant to be, at least not on that day.

Riding through Surprise, I saw several outdoor basketball courts. I would have stopped for a few minutes to watch, but no one was playing. Then I saw the sign, "Welcome to Tempe, All-American City." I had accomplished a major milestone!! I was four hundred and thirty two miles closer to the Atlantic Ocean!

The route took us through neighborhoods west of Phoenix, avoiding the busy streets. The settings were as I expected; beautifully manicured lawns and similar-looking stucco ranch homes lined the streets. The roads were smooth and clean. I did not see human activity. It was one hundred degrees, too hot for anyone to be outside.

I rode with Tom along the Arizona Canal Path for several miles. The canal runs parallel to the busy streets in the Phoenix Metro area. Tom and I were thrilled to be in Tempe, but we could not find the motel! My GPS directed me to a construction zone. We were stuck at a dead end along a waterway, trying to find a straightforward way to the other side of Salt River. Through trial and error, riding from one street to the next, backtracking often, we eventually found a bridge that connected us to the opposite side. I was beyond excited to be in Tempe. Dan and I roomed together at the Super 8 Motel on East Apache Boulevard, on the outskirts of the Arizona State University campus.

After settling into my room, I decided to walk toward the main campus. The area was buzzing with activity, students walking around—vastly different than the still neighborhoods I had ridden through an hour before. Electric scooters were prolific on the main campus. I did not know what to think of the large number of scooters that rivaled the number of cars on the roads. Most did not appear to be following any safety precautions as they sped through intersections, oblivious to vehicles or people passing through.

September 26 – Tempe (Rest Day)

My rest day began with a trip to Domenic's 2 Wheelers bike shop for a tune-up, the first of several on my journey. The folks who work in bicycle shops are committed, always pleasant, and exceptionally good at their craft. After enjoying coffee and a crumb cake at Starbucks, I decided to be productive and explore the city. First, a trip to the barbershop (a wonderful place to catch up on the local news, one of my favorite pastimes when visiting a new town or city). Afterward, I walked to Sun Devil Stadium for the highlight of my day. Pat Tillman played college football for ASU. He was drafted and played for the Arizona Cardinals in the NFL. His desire to put cause before himself after the 9/11 terrorist attacks drove him to give up his NFL career after three years and join the military. A true hero. He was killed in combat serving in Afghanistan in 2004.

It was late morning on Wednesday when I arrived at the Sun Devil Stadium's front entrance, a mile's walk from the Super 8 Motel. Except for construction workers, I did not see anyone I thought could help me figure out how to get into the stadium. I walked through a fenced-off area, entered the stadium complex, and made eye contact with a student working at the front desk. I introduced myself. "Hi, I'm Larry. I am with a group riding our bikes across the country. I love Pat Tillman's story, and I was wondering if there was any chance I could get a picture in front of the Tillman statue?"

Sydney, a junior at ASU, responded, "Sure, I could take you around the entire complex if you wanted me to."

I was psyched! "Yeah, I'd appreciate that very much!" Sydney walked me around the complex, pointing out highlights along the way. My very own docent! Sydney escorted me to the bronze, seven-foot-tall, four-hundred-pound Tillman statue in Sun Devil Stadium and showed me the mural, "A Grateful Nation," prominently displayed inside the Sun Devil football offices. The names and faces of every ASU football player and coach who ever wore the uniform are displayed on the large mural. ASU responded to the tragedy with unrestrained pride, turning parts of Sun Devil Stadium into a shrine of remembrance and reflection. I saw the wide receiver's team room; my son, Brian, plays the same position. Arizona State's tribute to Pat Tillman is grand. The school created a mural and named it Tillman's Tunnel, and it serves as an inspirational reminder of his sacrifice. Each Saturday afternoon, players pass through the tunnel and by the statue before entering the field during the season. I imagine it is a highly effective way to motivate players before a game. I was beyond thankful to Sydney for taking me behind the scenes.

On my walk back to the motel room, I reflected on the trip and life in general. Dipping my tires in the Pacific, crossing the Arizona border, and riding through the Imperial Sand Dunes in the California desert were all memorable. After hundreds of airplane rides ruminating about what it would be like to ride coast to coast, my dreams had become a reality.

When the bag of utensils fell off my bike about ten miles into the ride on the first full day, I wondered if I was up for the challenge. I was exhausted when I arrived at the Alpine campsite on the first night. When I set out the following morning after a good night of sleep, I knew I could do it. My outlook on life had changed entirely from three months before. I was full of energy, excited about meeting people and seeing unfamiliar places along the journey. By the time I entered Tempe, I had found my rhythm and started to think I was a good long-distance cyclist. I felt at ease and was so thankful I had acted on my desire to take on this challenge.

After an uplifting day in Tempe, it was time to continue our journey across the country. We were all rested and ready to go. I let Dan borrow an Army poncho liner I'd brought with me, because we expected the nights to become colder as we continued our trek east.

September 27 – Tempe to Usery Mountain Regional Park (25 miles)

The group left Tempe around 10:00 a.m. and began riding through East Valley neighborhoods en route to the Usery Mountains. Phoenix proper, known as the Valley of the Sun, is so named because Phoenix is flat and surrounded by mountain ranges on all sides. The mountains trap in smog, making Phoenix one of the United States' smoggiest cities.[8]

I rode by the Chicago Cubs' spring training ballpark, which triggered me to think about John, a friend in New Jersey who was originally from Chicago. He and his son Jack love the Cubs, Bears, and Bulls. I first met John (and his family) at the Mendham Borough Park when the circus came to town several years ago. My son and Jack are good friends. They spent a lot of time together growing up during their elementary and middle school years. I took a picture of the Cubs stadium and sent it to John and told him I was thinking about him. He texted me, acknowledging receipt of the photograph. Things along the route would trigger memories like that one and would occupy my mind for several minutes. Time and mileage added up as I lost myself in moments.

The Usery Mountain Regional Park, twenty miles east of Tempe, sat high above the Valley of the Sun. Phoenix was now a distant memory.

---

8   summitpost.org/phoenix-mountains-and-neighboring-ranges

From my perch, I was struck by the magnificence of the western vista. The sunsets and sunrises had been beautiful thus far, but nothing like the night we camped at Usery. At 6:44 p.m., I gazed to the west, and a skyline like no other appeared. A mixture of red, orange, and yellow blended to form a skyline appearing to be on fire, a sunset unique to the desert. The silhouette of a single cactus plant ten feet in front of where I stood conveyed the perfect mood for the occasion, a relaxed and contented group of cyclists. As soon as the sun dropped and darkness arrived, we settled inside our tents. The morning would come before we knew it.

September 28 – Usery Mountain Regional Park to Tonto Basin (67 miles)

The sunset was outdone only by the sunrise the next morning. I woke up at 4:45 a.m. and looked east and up to the sky that had started to lighten behind the mountains. The desert was quiet, the city and college town noise long gone—a setting difficult to replicate in the fast-paced world we live in today. Once again, another morning, I was energized to begin cycling again. (Of all the hundreds of pictures I took, the sunset and sunrise at Usery Mountain Regional Park resonate the most.)

As a kid in the 1960s, I was a huge fan of the Lone Ranger and his sidekick, Tonto. Playing cowboys and Indians was a favorite pastime. Sometimes I wanted to wear the handgun, holster, belt, and cowboy hat and pretend I was chasing down Indians. Cap guns brought everything to life. Other times I wanted to shoot a bow and arrow. It was okay to aim and shoot your "enemies" when I was growing up. It was all in fun—how times have changed. Over the next few days, we would ride through Apache Country. But first, we passed through Tonto Basin, Arizona. According to a National Public Radio story on the Lone Ranger, "Tonto Basin is the inspiration for Tonto, the Native American companion to the Lone Ranger."[9]

---

9   Kids.kiddle.co, Tonto_Basin_Arizona

I departed Usery Mountain Regional Park at six in the morning. Several cyclists were riding in my direction on the opposite side of the road. They were not carrying gear, so I assumed they were local cycling enthusiasts out for a morning ride before going to work. Before pedaling away from the park entrance, I looked at the ground. Directly in front of me was a huge tarantula. My mind at once flashed to 1985 when I was stationed at Fort Bliss, Texas. One weekend a lieutenant friend, his wife, and I took a trip to Carlsbad Caverns in New Mexico. As we approached the caverns, I looked out the window of my 1984 Honda Accord LX and saw a tarantula crossing the road. My friend told me tarantulas could jump five feet in the air. We were safe inside a car, so I did not think much of the comment. Flash forward to 2018. I stared at the motionless spider for a moment, snapped a picture, and then continued cycling. It is a myth that tarantulas can jump several feet in the air. But the thought entered my mind as I pedaled away.

The temperature rose to well over one hundred degrees once again, but there was a cool breeze to start the day. Cycling the first half of the day was extremely enjoyable. The skies brightened as the sun rose, peeking over the hills. The bright white circle surrounded by shades of yellow slowly rose to fill the sky with orange. It radiated a new beginning, the start of a brand-new day. And as the sunlight appeared, the mountains silhouetted against the backdrop of a rising sun transformed into jagged-edged peaks reaching for the sky. The tops of mountains came to life, then the lower half and the ground slowly turned from dark to light. The transformation was something to behold.

As morning turned to afternoon, traffic increased significantly on Highway 87; many cars and trucks sped past me. The steep mountains contributed to my changing attitude as the day wore on. The last forty miles before reaching Tonto Basin were agonizing; heat, hills, and traffic made for a tough finish to a long day.

Shortly after reaching the top of a mountain peak around Jakes Corner (elevation 4,565 feet), I surveyed the area. I could not tell if the specks I saw in the distance were small towns in the middle of the desert or a mixture of foliage, sagebrush, and cactus. I am confident I was standing on the spot I had seen from 35,000 feet on one of my cross-country flights in years past. Next time I am on a coast-to-coast flight and looking down from 35,000 feet, my reaction will be different. I will never again ponder what it's like riding on a bicycle through the barren wilderness.

We stayed at the Tonto Basin Inn right off Highway 188. The gravel parking lot was empty when I arrived midafternoon. I walked into the registration office to pick up my room key. The manager was watching TV on an old Sylvania set with an antenna protruding from the top. Time stood still. There was not a single item that I would categorize as a luxury. Folks live simple lives in this part of the country, vastly different from my hometown. My body was covered from head to toe in dirt and dust, adding a dark layer to my tanned, freckled skin that had been exposed to the sun for days on end. I showered, put my head on the pillow, closed my eyes, and waited for others to arrive.

The group walked along the highway to Big Daddy's Pizza half a mile from the inn. We were all so tired and famished. All we wanted to do was eat and sleep. The enormity of the day's accomplishment set in. We had just completed the most challenging cycling day so far: sixty-seven miles, 6,600 feet of climbing, temperatures above one hundred degrees, and the sun beating down all day. It was a very tough day on the saddle. It was pitch black when the group walked back to the inn after dinner, finally satisfied, but all of us feeling exhaustion and apprehension. No one spoke. We all knew the next few days would not be any easier.

September 29 – Tonto Basin to San Carlos Apache Indian Reservation (60 miles)

At breakfast, we learned that Dan was leaving the group. The day before, during the ride into Tonto Basin, he'd had difficulty navigating the steep descents. Even though his bike was retrofitted and had the benefit of two sets of brakes, keeping control of his bicycle loaded with equipment with one arm proved extremely difficult. I could only imagine, since I had difficulty keeping control using both of my arms. He brought so much energy and personality to the group. But safety was first and foremost. After contemplating the situation, he had decided to return home to Southern California. We all wished him well, then packed and continued our trek east. Honestly, riding a bike, fully loaded, across the country with one arm is an incredible feat. He is an inspiration to all to keep pushing ahead and make the best of every day. I think about Dan quite a bit. I know there was a reason I met him.

I was excited to leave Tonto Basin because our next destination was a campsite on an Apache Reservation. I had not seen a body of water since leaving San Diego, 520 miles west of this location. That was about to change. In the distance, about twenty miles southeast of Tonto Basin, riding on Arizona Route 188, I saw sparkling water. The rising sun shone down onto Theodore Roosevelt Lake, the oldest and largest artificial reservoir in Arizona. The surrounding landscape was striking; a series of mountain ranges in the background, clear blue skies, and crystal-clear sparkling water made for exquisite pictures. I thought about the challenges faced by local communities keeping a water supply to survive. Accessing a simple luxury, like clean water, widely available in urban and suburban settings, is more complicated for people who live in the Arizona communities I rode through. In the distance, I saw a couple of boats along the shoreline. The reservoir was a perfect peaceful vacation destination, especially for those traveling by RV.

Before leaving Tempe, we met a guy at the Super 8 Motel who recommended that we be careful riding through the Apache Reservation. He alluded to instances when cyclists had reported being harassed by people in cars looking to make trouble with outsiders. The guy did not seem paranoid to me. I made a mental note. But I did wonder why he felt the need to share that information with us.

I made it to the San Carlos Apache Indian Reservation shortly before dusk and pitched my tent in a vacant area next to a casino. Since Arizona is home to rattlesnakes, Gila monsters, black widows, tarantulas, and scorpions, I always checked inside my tent before entering at night. I also checked inside my shoes and shook my clothing before dressing in the morning. I slept with the tent zippers fully closed. You never knew what type of critter might pay a visit in the middle of the night. We ate a buffet dinner inside the casino. It was not very crowded, about fifty percent capacity.

The Penn State–Ohio State football game was televised in the bar area. I watched Penn State lose after holding a decent lead. I am a die-hard Penn State fan, but, surprisingly, I was not yelling at the TV like I usually did back home. It was effortless for me to avoid television, and I rarely checked the news on my iPhone during the entire trip across the country. It felt so good to mostly disconnect from the negative stories that were dominating the news cycle every day.

I saw more horses and cattle than people. Convenience stores rarely sold fresh produce. On the reservation, teenagers hung out around a convenience store I stopped at, smoking cigarettes. I wondered why they were not in school. One teenage kid smiled at me. The teeth I saw, separated by gaps, were crooked and brown; it did not look like he had ever been to a dentist. It made me sad to see how people lived on the reservation. Despair. Poverty. Simple living. These are some of the thoughts that entered my mind as I rode.

I considered what it would take to help these communities thrive. All the simple solutions leaders talk about did not seem to make any sense. I wondered if giving more money to the problems was the answer. I do not believe there is a solution that currently exists. Waiting (or hoping) for the all-knowing politician to arrive with the magic wand is futile—it will not happen, despite all the promises. On the surface are the obvious issues: lack of education, lack of health care, a long history of reliance on government, and the usual leeches that work the system to enrich themselves at the expense of rural communities such as Native American reservations. I am curious how many politicians have ever spent considerable time in this part of the country.

One idea entered my mind, and I thought about it quite a bit as I rode through the reservation: All future leaders in Congress should spend months living in a community that is different than their own. If a congressperson from the Northeast who attended an Ivy League school and law school (no military service) spent time living among the population on an Indian reservation, they would be more likely to reflect on any decision they made with care and concern for all people. I also thought about the Electoral College. Getting rid of it would marginalize these small communities even more than they already are. The solutions needed to elevate these communities out of poverty are complicated and require more effort and creative thinking than we see today.

Our route across the country was not a straight line. For many days we rode north and then south to get over mountains before riding east. I remember thinking Florida was east of us, so that was the direction I wanted to ride! Today, we began riding due east. Every mile completed was one mile closer to St. Augustine. Riding through the desert requires different thinking; the word "essential" takes on a completely new meaning. Simple things matter. Food. Water. Shelter. A fully functioning bicycle. Sunscreen. Sunglasses. Paper maps in case technologies falter.

I was thrilled to be riding all alone in the Arizona desert—and a little anxious, not knowing whether I could fix my bike if a mechanical problem derailed me. I wanted to put myself in an uncomfortable environment to test myself. Still, I did not know if I could deal with the consequences of injury, mechanical problems, or a significant weather event. This cognitive dissonance played out in my mind as I rode through the Apache Reservation in the Arizona desert.

September 30 – San Carlos Apache Indian Reservation to Safford (73 miles)

The Southern Tier route passed through the town of Pima, Arizona. For cross-country cyclists, entering Pima is important. According to ACA lore, Pima Taylor Freeze sold the best ice cream on the entire journey. The simple things in life! I was energized, knowing a treat awaited me after hours of riding in the blazing hot sun. I became more excited when I saw the sign "Entering Pima." I felt like a kid going out for ice cream on a summer night, like one of those nights my parents took the family to Carvel as a reward for behaving in church.

It was a complete letdown when I saw the "Closed" sign. Bummer! Nevertheless, I rested on a bench in front of the store and treated myself to a bottle of Gatorade. Riding on US Route 70, also known as the Old West Highway, brought me back to what it must have been like to live in this area over one hundred years ago. I imagined Indian tribes roaming the countryside on horseback. I wondered how they navigated, survived. There were not any road signs to follow, that's for sure. The landscape all looked the same. Mountains in the distance. The desert floor. Horses and cattle roaming. Everything exposed to the elements.

I stopped at the Apache Burger Travel Center on Highway 70 in Peridot, Arizona. The lady behind the counter smiled and said, "Good morning." I smiled and nodded to express my gratitude for the nice welcome. I always made it a point to buy a drink or snack, whether I needed to replenish it or not. Often, I filled my CamelBak with ice for no charge. I loved conversing with people I met along the way. I would usually have a five- or ten-minute conversation, and then I would continue riding. I asked about their day and what I could expect on the road ahead; they were always curious to know about the ride, where I was from, et cetera. I often received a hearty goodbye and a wish for safe travels. Geronimo's picture hung on the wall next to the store entrance, with the inscription "Chief of the Notorious Band of Arizona Apache Indians. Photo by Ed Irwin – 1847."

When I saw Eastern Arizona College's welcome sign, it hit me: I had nearly crossed the entire state of Arizona! People were milling around, and there was quite a bit of rush hour traffic in downtown Safford when I arrived at about 6:00 p.m. I sensed a shift in the terrain. Brown dirt with mountains in the background morphed into green grass, pastures, and trees all around. Clouds formed in the sky, and rain was in the forecast for this night. The humidity crept up, which meant mosquitos would be out in force.

An employee from the State of Arizona, responsible for improving cyclists' road safety, joined our group after dinner. She was aware that the Adventure Cycling Southern Tier route passed through Arizona. She asked for feedback on our experience riding through her state. We were brutally honest and suggested removing debris from road surfaces and pruning shrubs protruding onto the road shoulders. Overgrowth often forced me to move onto the road, increasing concern about vehicles sneaking up from behind and clipping my bike. The person she replaced had focused his efforts on developing road cycling standard operating procedures (SOPs). Her task was to implement the SOPs with a mandate to enhance the cycling experience.

We celebrated Joyce's sixtieth birthday on this night. Joyce, one of two women in the group, was leading her first cross-country bike tour. She'd recently retired from the National Park Service and was a current member of the Adventure Cycling Association Executive Council. She had ridden her bike from Oregon to San Diego to lead our group across the country.

Chapter 3

NEW MEXICO (SILVER CITY, EMORY PASS, AND HEADWINDS)

October 1 – Safford to Lordsburg (76 miles)

I crossed the border into New Mexico shortly after leaving Safford. I rode on Highway 70, traversing the narrow passes of the Whitlock Mountains, and entered the Black Hills before descending into Duncan, New Mexico. The combination of the slight tailwind, the drop from 4,400 feet to 3,600 feet, and the smoothly paved and lightly traveled road were the perfect ingredients, setting the stage for an amazing cycling experience. Unrestrained, I averaged eighteen miles per hour for an hour of cycling, with an unprecedented adrenaline rush as I cut through the breeze in the tuck position, rivaled only by the thrilling sensations experienced on a favorite roller coaster ride. That last twenty miles into Duncan was the first time I truly let loose. I had become accustomed to Tank and felt extremely comfortable exceeding forty miles per hour.

I entered Duncan and immediately saw a sign honoring its hometown hero, Sandra Day O'Connor. This old Western town offered a glimpse into its past, a setting that left me feeling I knew what it was like to live here a hundred years before. Reminiscent of the wild, wild West was a condemned wooden building with a marquee sign that still read "Saloon" hanging over swinging wooden doors. I imagined drunk cowboys coming face to face in front of the saloon, only one surviving the eventual duel. I envisioned the inside looking eerily similar to the setting of the duel between Jimmy (Gregory Peck) and Eddie in the 1950 film *The Gunfighter*. Eddie, not impressed with the legend of Jimmy, who had entered the saloon and was standing at the bar, confronts him, taunts him, and eventually is silenced by him. I imagined that was how scores were settled in Duncan, New Mexico, many years before.

I rested for about thirty minutes at the Stage Stop mini-mart and gas station. There was a horse and buggy logo underneath the Stage Stop sign, a not-so-subtle reminder of the town's proud history. Train tracks, the Gila River, and a handful of old pickup trucks dotted the area. Everybody pumping gas or walking into the store seemed to know each other. It had a small-town friendly vibe. I spoke to a resident who knew Sandra Day O'Connor. I thought about the hurdles she faced growing up and how she overcame insurmountable odds to land on the Supreme Court. I met a couple of bikers resting at the gas station, standing next to their Harley-Davidson motorcycles. I enjoyed all my conversations. Meeting good folks in the heart of America kept me going and searching for the next surprise.

Unfortunately, the last thirty-six miles were not as much fun as the first forty. I battled tremendous headwinds riding toward Lordsburg, New Mexico, on Highway 70. A storm passed ahead of me as I approached the town. I could see for miles. Ominous-looking clouds and dust funnels appeared over the landscape. As I got closer to the squall, I searched for a place to shelter. I began to feel the effects of the storm. Ground debris began swirling around. I was out of luck, no place to shelter. I kept pedaling and hoped for the best. I eventually arrived at the KOA campsite, having been spared the worst of the storm. Joel, who rode point (at the head of the group), got pelted with hail about three miles in front of me. Thankfully, we both arrived in one piece. We pitched our tents at the campsite in Lordsburg and waited for the rest of the group to arrive.

After pitching my tent, I flipped my bike over, spun each tire, and ran my fingers along the tread, looking and feeling for any sharp object. Sure enough, I pulled a piece of steel out of my back tire. It was the third time I had found a piece of steel. Surprisingly, my tire had kept the proper air pressure: 80 PSI. By now, everyone else in the group had experienced at least one flat tire. A couple had had multiple flats. My technique seemed to be working well. I paid close attention to the road, avoided debris as much as possible, and performed necessary maintenance twice a day.

My military training came in handy. As a soldier, I spent many days in the garrison (the physical location of the fort), working at the battalion motor pool (the site where equipment is kept) performing maintenance on essential equipment. Soldiers did not want to fail an unannounced inspection by the company first sergeant (the top noncommissioned enlisted person in charge of a military company-size unit). Failing an inspection could result in a soldier's losing a privilege, such as being restricted to the barracks or receiving KP duty, a punishment everyone tried to avoid. So they took vehicle maintenance seriously. Ingrained in every soldier's brain was that one can never perform enough maintenance.

Upgrading to Schwalbe Marathon Plus tires, which prevent punctures better than Continental tires do, was a wise decision. I had also added sealant (glue) inside the inner tubes. With any minor puncture, the glue plugs the hole, keeping air from escaping. That is the theory. It worked well! I noticed others in the group, much more experienced than I was, starting to flip their bikes to check tires after arriving at camp. This inexperienced long-distance cyclist had a few tricks up his sleeve and was willing to share.

October 2 – Lordsburg to Silver City (46 miles)

The first time I heard of puncture vines was when I crossed the border into New Mexico. Puncture vines grow in dry climates where few other plants can survive.[10] The vines drop goatheads, burs that have long, sharp spines that easily penetrate tires. I kept a watchful eye, on the lookout for goatheads, for the next several hundred miles. I felt anxious riding through much of New Mexico and Texas, not knowing if I would inadvertently ride over these tire killers. I could not relax like I wanted to. I was always looking down to the right side of my bike, trying to avoid anything that looked like it did not belong on a road shoulder.

An empty basketball court caught my attention right before I exited the Lordsburg KOA campground. Seeing the court, I reflected on my journey: injuring my foot, losing my job, which triggered a downward spiral, and then taking up cycling to help kick-start my focused effort to get my life back on track. The game I loved and could not play was a catalyst fueling my desire to take on this epic journey.

The temperature dropped a few degrees after the storm passed through Lordsburg. Thankfully, we no longer dealt with temperatures over one hundred degrees. We all looked forward to a well-deserved rest day in Silver City, New Mexico, which was known for silver, gold, copper, lead, and zinc.

I had rarely paid attention to the RV community before starting this cross-country ride. My brother-in-law Mike and his wife, Pam, travel the country in their RV, riding from state to state to visit family and see new and interesting places. The idea of RVing had never connected with me. It just seemed like too much work for limited benefit. But on this trip, I began to change my tune. I watched families gather outside their RVs under the stars next to a campfire. Kids played while adults mingled and had an enjoyable time. RVs ranged from van-size to much larger, some with fully extendable rear and side porches. High-end RVs can

---

10 Nazinvasiveplants.org

cost hundreds of thousands of dollars. I can now see myself traveling the western part of the United States in an RV (of a size I could confidently drive and afford).

New Mexico roads are excellent for cycling. They are smooth and freshly paved, but road shoulders are virtually nonexistent. Even so, I felt comfortable riding in the traffic lane, especially at speeds approaching thirty-five or forty miles per hour. On this day, I was ready to tackle another 3,500-foot climb before descending into Silver City. Just before crossing the Continental Divide, I saw a cyclist riding west. She was cruising fast downhill. We said hello to each other but did not stop to chat. Usually, if the road is flat, both riders will stop and talk for a few minutes. In the hills, it's a different situation. Just wave and keep going. As I descended into Silver City at high speed, three wild boars ran in front of me. I saw them well in advance as they started to enter the highway on the opposite side of the road. They nonchalantly ran by and disappeared into the woods. I never felt I was in danger. This sighting was not my first time seeing a wild boar. I flashed back to 1990, when I performed military maneuvers at Fort Hunter Liggett, located one hour south of Salinas, California. This place I called home from 1989 to 1991 was brought to life by John Steinbeck in his book *East of Eden*. I routinely rode by teams of wild boar in my Humvee while on these military maneuvers. I remember seeing many more than three in a group.

We arrived at Silver City by 6:00 p.m. It was my night to cook. However, the group thought it would be a clever idea to eat at the Jalisco Café on Bullard Street, a highly recommended Mexican restaurant in downtown Silver City. The decision was unanimous. The restaurant served the best chicken enchiladas! On the way back to our campsite, I stopped at the Food Basket, a local grocery store that was two tenths of a mile from the RV park, to buy breakfast and lunch items for our rest day. The cook always selected the menu items. Whenever I cooked and carried the credit card, Double Stuf Oreos and vanilla ice cream always made it into the shopping cart.

October 3 – Silver City (Rest Day)

I called Martin, owner of Gila Hike & Bike, the day before arriving in Silver City to inquire about store hours. He assured me mechanics were ready to help when my cycling group arrived in town. I enjoyed visiting bike shops. I felt a connection with the employees after getting to know the folks at Whippany Cycle in New Jersey before leaving for my journey. In the morning, I dropped off my bike at the shop for a tune-up. The rear tire tread had borne the brunt of the six-hundred-mile journey from San Diego and had worn down much more than the front tire, so they rotated them. I bought two twenty-five-ounce CamelBak insulated water bottles; the non-insulated bottles I'd brought were not well suited for the desert heat. In the desert, cold drinking water turned to warm bathwater within minutes. Martin, Erica, the mechanic, and the rest of the Gila Hike & Bike shop crew went out of their way to ensure I was ready to continue my journey. I took care of other errands, including visiting the local barbershop, laundromat, and post office to ship nonessential items home.

I took in all that Silver City offered. I visited Billy the Kid's home site and the jail he escaped from when he lived in Silver City in the 1860s. I am used to seeing bigger cities full of activity and people roaming the streets, but this was not the case in Silver City. Many of the people I met there reminded me of those who live in the Southern states, where folks do things a little slower than in the hectic, fast-paced Northeastern section of the country. I saw the American flag flying high, proud, and often—a not-so-subtle reminder that I was indeed riding through our great United States of America.

There is no better place to catch up on the local news than in a small-town barbershop. Leroy, the barber at the downtown Silver Clipper Barbershop, was originally from Brooklyn. He told me the extent of his long-distance cycling was riding his bike across the Brooklyn Bridge. Leroy is one of the few African Americans I saw outside of San Diego or Tempe, along the six-hundred-mile stretch since leaving San Diego on September 17.

I met Steve at the local Army surplus store on the main street. Military clothing, equipment, and other paraphernalia were scattered on coat racks, shelves, and tables, a hodge-podge of items that had fueled the family store for two generations. Steve told me he was one of six brothers—the only one who did not ship off to Vietnam. His story reminded me of the movie *Saving Private Ryan*. Initially, I enjoyed the conversation with Steve, but after a few minutes of friendly chatter, he told me about a neighbor who'd recently moved next to his property outside of town. He spoke badly about his new neighbor, using the F-word to the point where I stopped the conversation and left the store. I told him it was nice to meet him, and I walked out. I wondered how his business thrived with the way he talked to potential customers—very odd behavior.

I met Wayne, a frail-looking World War II veteran walking with a cane, in the Food Basket grocery store when I was food shopping. He wore a West Point cap. I introduced myself and asked him about the hat and his connection to West Point. He told me his neighbor had graduated from the Academy and always made it a point to visit him when he returned home. Wayne served on the *USS Sausalito*, one of our nation's finest.

Meeting Wayne brought back memories of the night I joined VFW Post 7858 in Bernardsville, New Jersey, in 2013. I introduced myself to the members and shared a brief history of my military background. One of the qualifiers for membership into the VFW is service in a war, campaign, or expedition on foreign soil or hostile waters. My eligibility came from my year serving in Korea and my deployment to Panama during Operation Just Cause. At the end of the meeting, an older VFW member approached me and asked about my time in Korea. I served in 1987–1988, not during the Korean War in 1950–1953 when he was there. I am immensely proud that I honorably served our nation, but my time in Korea was hardly comparable to the experience of my comrade.

The sacrifices my parents' generation made were remarkable. I wish today's younger generation aspired to be more like the Greatest Generation.

Anticipation was building as our climb to Emory Pass, the highest peak on the Southern Tier, was only a couple of days away. After a day of rest in Silver City, it was time to continue our trek.

I passed many historical markers on the highways in Arizona and New Mexico. At first, I stopped at all of them to read the inscriptions. I was curious to learn about the history of the areas I rode through. The most common stories dealt with Apaches and settlers going into battle. One such incident's road marker near Silver City, New Mexico, tells the story of the McComas family. A couple, the McComases, were killed by a group of Apaches toward the end of the Apache Wars.[11] After I departed Silver City, and until I reached St. Augustine, I was selective, only stopping to read a marker if, at the previous night's map meeting, Joyce mentioned something was worth reading. My cycling rhythm was disrupted every time I stopped. I did not like that. Goodbye, Silver City. Up next was Mimbres, New Mexico.

October 4 – Silver City to Mimbres (28 miles)

About thirty minutes after leaving Silver City, I rode by the Santa Rita mine, the third-oldest active open-pit copper mine in the world. I also rode past the Kneeling Nun, which I could barely make out in the distance. The Kneeling Nun is a monolith in the Santa Rita Mountains that rises over five hundred feet and resembles a human in a kneeling position. According to an article that appeared in the *Silver City Daily Press*, the Kneeling Nun legend goes back to the early days of the Spanish conquest of Mexico.

Men under Coronado's command came through the area searching for gold. Monks and nuns also came and built a monastery. The conquerors had conflicts with the Apaches. (Santa Rita was the heart

---

11 Waymarking.com

of Apache Country.) The wounded were brought to the monastery to be treated and tended to by the nuns. One of the nuns, Sister Rita, fell in love with an injured soldier that she had nursed back to health. Sister Rita was sentenced to die after their love was discovered. "Instead of death, she prayed to be turned into a stone, and she was."[12]

The tops of the Santa Rita Mountains were totally sheared off. There was a striking contrast between the Santa Rita Mountains, which could serve as a makeshift mountain airplane landing strip, and the jagged peaks dominating the Arizona wilderness. I made out tiny trucks on top of the mountains and powering up the roads leading to the top. From my vantage point, the trucks looked like Tonka trucks silhouetted against the massive mountain backdrop. I stopped and put on my GoPro camera before descending into the valley as I made my way to Mimbres. I wanted to capture the fantastic experience of cycling through the mountains and maneuvering the switchbacks, the paths cutting sharply from one direction to the other. I was surrounded by the Kneeling Nun (at 7,563 feet elevation) to the south of me, and Hermosa Mountain (7,576 feet) and Hanover Mountain (7,521 feet) to the north of me on my way to Mimbres, which is nestled in the south end of Bear Canyon.

For the first couple of days after leaving San Diego, I attached the GoPro to my chest. I believed I could capture the best videos from that vantage point. After taking a couple of short videos, I realized my body position did not align as well with the GoPro as I wanted. I needed to figure out a better place to attach it. The more significant issue was that attaching the GoPro to my chest made breathing more difficult. I eventually settled on attaching it underneath my helmet like a beanie. Pictures were much clearer, less choppy, and gave the viewer a better appreciation of the bona fide experience. The problem was that after a few minutes with it attached to my helmet, I began to experience headaches. Eventually, I settled on attaching my GoPro underneath my helmet, but only periodically and for limited times.

---

12 Silver City Daily Press, "A piece of history," (Thompson, June 9, 2018)

I am glad I snapped hundreds of pictures and several hours of videos. Occasionally, I watch them to relive certain aspects of the journey. I cut down the large volume of film and photos to an enjoyable one-hour video reel synced to some great music. My trip is now documented for future Walsh generations to enjoy.

The final five-mile ride into Mimbres exceeded my expectations. I rode in the middle of the highway, approaching forty miles per hour. I navigated the switchbacks in the tucked racing position. The ride was intoxicating, weaving back and forth through the mountain maze. The rush I felt was similar to that of the first six seconds of free fall after jumping out the side door of a US Air Force C-130 airplane, before the parachute opens.

I was the first to arrive at the Mimbres campsite in early afternoon. I set up my tent and then walked to the office to chat with the RV park manager. It did not take long for me to recognize a familiar Massachusetts accent. I felt connected with her, because my parents grew up in Massachusetts. Another couple joined the office manager and her husband for an afternoon social gathering. The TV was tuned to Fox News.

It was my turn to cook again. I walked to the Valle Mimbres Market, a fruit and vegetable market, about a quarter mile from the campsite. Joyce joined me. I bought a few dinner items. I wondered how stores like this were able to remain open. I could not imagine how the local community could support this store, which sold produce, drinks, and other staples. I picked up noodles, meatballs, and tomato sauce. Yes, pasta and a salad were on the menu once again. We ate a hearty meal.

The temperature had dropped to the high forties in the last few days. After dinner and the map meeting, I decided to call it a night earlier than usual. The lore of Emory Pass had weighed heavily on the group the past couple of days, and we were expecting the big ascent first thing in the morning. We camped under the stars, preparing for our big climb. No two days had been alike since we dipped our tires into the Pacific Ocean. It was the experience of a lifetime that everyone should have the opportunity to pursue.

October 5 – Mimbres to Caballo (53 miles)

After breakfast was over and the bikes were packed, everyone was quiet, busy making last-minute mechanical adjustments. Everyone left at a different time—unusual behavior and not the typical morning departure routine. I wore a long-sleeve Smartwool top underneath my short-sleeve cycling shirt. Choosing the proper cycling attire for my upper torso was always a challenge for me, and particularly on days like today. The combination of perspiration, wind, and temperature changes all contributed to my never-ending clothing assessment.

Surrounded by a striking blue sky and a crisp morning calm at 8:13 a.m., I was ready to go. About halfway up the nineteen-mile climb on Highway 152, I became anxious about my surroundings. Cars and trucks were few and far between. The climb was steep. Pedaling was my focus until I heard rustling in the brush. I immediately thought about mountain lions. They are known to live in the mountain regions of New Mexico. Stalking is normal behavior for them. I reminded myself of where I kept a small knife and a horn I used to startle dogs (aggressive dogs run wild in eastern Texas and western Louisiana). A couple of miles later, from a new vantage point, I concluded that whatever was out there was no longer a threat.

As I approached the top of Emory Pass, the wind started to pick up, and the temperature dropped significantly. Pine trees dominated both sides of the highway leading to the top. The smell of pine and the surrounding landscape reminded me of the Santa Cruz Mountains in California. Kelley and I had spent a lot of time in the Santa Cruz mountains in the early 1990s. After getting married, we'd hosted a wedding reception in Ben Lomond, a town nestled in the Santa Cruz Mountains, for friends who could not make our wedding in Detroit.

At 10:57 a.m., about two hundred yards before reaching the top, I stopped to admire the scenery. I looked behind me far in the distance over the endless mountains. The wind cut through my clothing and chilled my body. I thought it was cool that my body had propelled me on the saddle of Tank to this point, Emory Pass. I had imagined many times before what it would be like to reach the summit.

Grinding out the last fifty yards to the summit on Highway 152 in the granny gear (the smallest cog on the front crankset; when used, one can easily pedal at walking speed), I rounded the last tight, steep switchback, expecting the big reveal. And there it was, up ahead about fifteen yards. As I approached the Emory Pass historical marker, the wind increased, and when I finally arrived at the summit, the wind howled. The vast expansive landscape on the backside captured my attention. Reaching the summit was a relief. It had not been as difficult as I thought it would be, except for the last half mile before the summit. However, the breathtaking panoramic views exceeded my wildest expectations.

One dramatic vista I photographed is reminiscent of the 1948 photo by Ansel Adams titled *Mount Moran, Autumn, Grand Teton National Park, Wyoming*, except the sky was blue, not grey. It was a view the likes of which I had never seen before. Joel arrived about five minutes after I did. We leaned our bikes next to the Emory Pass sign and took a few pictures for posterity's sake. One car zoomed past us, heading west. A man wearing hiking clothing and carrying a heavy-duty hiking stick walked past us and into the woods. I wanted to enjoy the moment, but it was cold and windy, so we decided to continue down the backside of Emory Pass after a thirty-minute break.

The wind died down on the backside of the summit. The mountains came alive with color. A clear blue sky above and cloud cover in the distance merged to form a line across the sky on the horizon. Underneath it all, I saw a series of mountain ranges. I felt like I was on top of the world. I could see for miles. For all I knew, the furthest mountains were in a different state.

It was a much faster ride down the other side of the mountain. I applied the brakes on and off for most of the descent. My forearms burned as I weaved in and out of switchbacks, going between thirty-five and forty miles per hour the entire way. The excitement and anticipation of ascending to the summit of Emory Pass had come and gone. This moment of jubilation quickly turned to a feeling of wanting. Another accomplishment, another milestone met. I wondered what was next.

Doug, Tom, and I stopped at a café in the small village of Hillsboro near the bottom of the mountain. (Tom, retired and living in Virginia Beach, Virginia, had completed the 4,200-mile TransAmerica Route, in the same tour group as Wally, a month before joining our group in San Diego.) Most of the males who entered the café wore cowboy hats, and trucks lined the street and dominated the small café parking lot. It was the type of place where everyone in town congregates on a Saturday morning to eat breakfast and catch up on the local news.

After the rest break in Hillsboro, I continued riding to the base of the mountain; I got a glimpse of the vast wilderness to the east. With a favorable wind, I decided to see how fast I could ride a ten-mile segment. I put my head down and, for the next ten miles, I turned Highway 152 into my very own racetrack. I rode as fast as I could and mustered enough energy to average 24.42 miles per hour, the fastest ten-mile average speed of my entire trip. I was in the desert all alone, pedaling as hard as I could. There were no distractions, just my burning leg muscles and the thought that I would have a good night's sleep.

I did not see any vehicles whatsoever driving on the recently paved desert highway. Smooth black asphalt roads, a clearly marked yellow centerline, and a thick white line separating a broad road shoulder set the tone for a unique riding experience. Unlike Pennsylvania, the Pothole State, the roads in the western part of the United States are exposed to less extreme temperature changes, resulting in less contracting and fewer potholes. The human activity I did see—several adults unloading all-terrain vehicles from the beds of pickup trucks—appeared to be getting ready to have some fun riding in ideal terrain for off-road activity. On some days, unforgiving winds and unpredictable weather made riding on highways more dangerous than I wished. But today, my mind was free from any safety concern whatsoever.

The Caballo campsite is exposed to the violent sand-laden desert wind from the north, south, and west and is buttressed by the Caballo Reservoir and the Caballo Mountains to the east. Truth or Consequences, a town famous for choosing to rename itself after the Truth or Consequences radio show,[13] is thirteen miles south of the Caballo campsite. Temperature and wind extremes are characteristic of most deserts, including this campsite in the Northern Chihuahuan Desert. The wind started howling within an hour after I arrived, and the temperature quickly dropped. I secured my tent with extra stakes and placed heavy rocks on each of the tent corners for extra stability. One lonely horse grazed across the street in the vast barren desert surrounded by tumbleweeds and stone—a scene reminiscent of old Western movies when cowboys or Indians appear out of nowhere galloping on horseback in the wilderness. I wondered if the horse was wild or domesticated.

I bought snacks and drinks from the campground's general store. The campground manager was from Harrisburg, Pennsylvania, near where I grew up, and graduated from a rival high school. In a matter of two days, I had met a retiree from Massachusetts and another from Pennsylvania. Not everyone from the Northeast retires to Florida.

Even though I was away from my family, separated by two thousand miles, I felt connected because of Facebook. Kelley had everything under control at home, so I could concentrate fully on finishing the ride. I do not think it would have been possible for me to complete it if I had not had unconditional support from my family before and during the ride.

I had lost a lot of weight by the time I made it to Emory Pass. My waistline decreased from size 38 to 36. The excess fat around my waist dwindled as my body reshaped itself. I thought I could get that six-pack back. The excess length of belt on my cargo pants dangled more and more as each day passed.

---

13 Newmexico.org.articles.post

I took it one day at a time and chose not to total up the miles after each day on the saddle. I thought doing so would have been like watching paint dry, unimportant and menial, and not worth the effort. However, lying in my tent at the Caballo campground, I decided to tally miles and feet climbed, the first time since leaving San Diego nineteen days earlier. Wow! I had ridden 860 miles and climbed 37,083 feet so far. "Oh my God, I cycled higher than Mount Everest!" I mused. The notion of climbing to the top of the world struck me as cool.

SECTION 1
San Diego, CA to Tempe, AZ
417.5 Miles

San Diego • Tempe

St. Augustine

- Route Map and Guide
- Bi-Directional
- Services for Cyclists
- Waterproof Paper

Sept. 17, 2018 – Dog Beach, Pacific Ocean-San Diego

Sept. 17, 2018 – Dog Beach, Deb and Gary foreground, Joel and Joyce background

Sept. 18, 2018 – Alpine campsite, Alpine, California

Sept. 19, 2018 – The Wall, Jacumba Hot Springs, California

Sept. 21, 2018 – Imperial Sand Dunes, California

*Sept. 21, 2018
Good Samaritan at border
station, Brawley, California*

Sept. 22, 2018 – California and Arizona Border, Ehrenberg, Arizona

Sept. 23, 2018 – Dan and Larry, preparing to leave Quartzsite, Arizona

Sept. 25, 2018
Tom riding on the
Arizona Canal Bike Path,
Phoenix, Arizona

Sept. 26, 2018
Pat Tillman Statue inside
ASU Sun Devils Stadium,
Tempe, Arizona

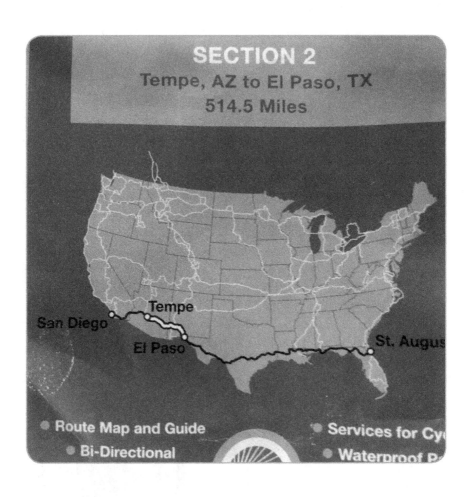

SECTION 2
Tempe, AZ to El Paso, TX
514.5 Miles

San Diego
Tempe
El Paso
St. Augus

● Route Map and Guide ● Services for Cy●
● Bi-Directional ● Waterproof P●

Sept. 27, 2018 – Sunset at Usery Mountain Regional Park, Arizona

Sept. 28, 2018 – Sunrise at Usery Mountain Regional Park, Arizona

Sept. 29, 2018 – Roosevelt Lake, 11 miles SE of Tonto Basin, Arizona

Sept. 30, 2018
Old West Highway
(Highway 70),
Pima, Arizona

Sept. 30, 2018 – Celebrating Joyce's birthday, Tom in background, Safford, Arizona

Oct. 1, 2018 – Riding into storm on Highway 70, Lordsburg, New Mexico

Oct. 2, 2018
Shopping at Food Basket in
Silver City, New Mexico

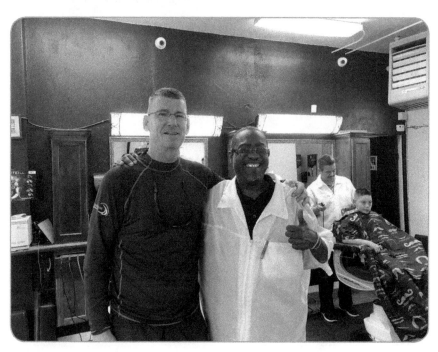

Oct. 3, 2018 – Silver Clipper Barber Shop, Silver City, New Mexico

Oct. 4, 2018 – The Kneeling Nun (Santa Rita Mountains),
Highway 152, San Lorenzo, New Mexico

Oct. 5, 2018
Emory Pass, Gila
National Forest, Highway
152, New Mexico

Oct. 7, 2018 – Rio Grande, Highway 28 west of Las Cruces, New Mexico

Oct. 7, 2018 – The Killer Rabbit – on a dirt path near Canutillo, Texas

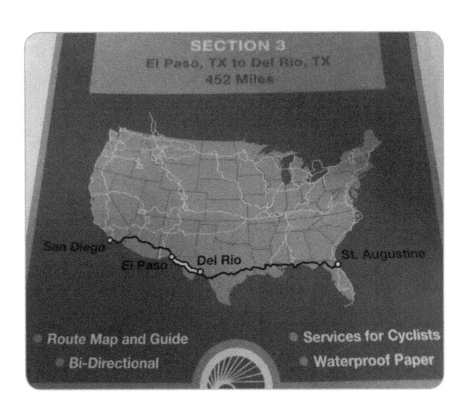

SECTION 3
El Paso, TX to Del Rio, TX
452 Miles

San Diego

El Paso   Del Rio

St. Augustine

● Route Map and Guide   ● Services for Cyclists
  ● Bi-Directional   ● Waterproof Paper

Oct. 8, 2018 – Carrying food to the Fort Hancock, Texas community church

Oct. 10, 2018 – Prada desert display 30 miles west of Marfa, Texas on Highway 90

*Oct. 10, 2018 – Joel pedaling to a phantom hill crest
in the Texas desert on Highway 90*

Oct. 10, 2018 – Train traveling on the Union Pacific Railroad on Texas Highway 90

Oct. 11, 2018 – Haircut in Marfa, Texas

Oct. 11, 2018 – Enjoying a night out in Marfa, Texas

Oct. 13, 2018 – Sunrise on Highway 90 between Marathon and Sanderson, Texas

Oct. 14, 2018 – Entering the twilight zone on Highway 90 near Dryden, Texas

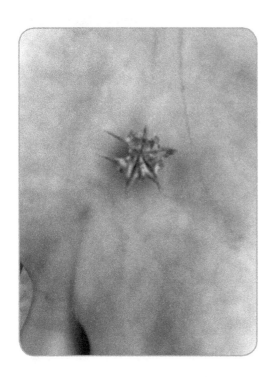

Sept. 29, 2018
San Carlos Apache Reservation
near Bylas, Arizona – goathead

Sept. 20, 2018
Somewhere in California –
tiny piece of steel

Chapter 4

TEXAS (IT IS A BIG STATE!)

October 6 and 7 – Caballo to Las Cruces (63 miles) to El Paso (54 miles)

When I left the campsite at 8:00 a.m., the temperature was a chilly fifty degrees, and Highway 187 was quiet and clear of traffic. I rode by an empty Caballo Tavern parking lot, too early for happy hour, and shortly after, I reached the fully operational Riggs Chili Company in Arrey, New Mexico. In front of the main building, a large dump truck unloaded chili peppers onto a conveyor belt, which transported them to another conveyor belt before they disappeared inside the processing plant. I could see the bright red peppers moving swiftly from my vantage point about a hundred yards away, and I wondered how many restaurants this one processing plant supplied.

I did not expect dogs to start chasing me for a few hundred miles (according to the ACA's Southern Tour description, aggressive dog encounters occurred in eastern Texas and western Louisiana). Well, I was wrong. About eight-thirty that morning, when riding alone, minding my own business, I heard a barking dog on the left side of the road. I had prepared for this moment since the first time I read about the Southern Tier route. The dog started running toward me. I pushed the button on the dog horn attached to my front handlebar. It did not make a sound. I pressed again. It still did not work. I pedaled harder to quicken my pace, realizing the dog was coming right for me. Luckily, it stopped in its tracks at its owner's property line. I'd avoided contact during my first aggressive dog encounter. But there would be plenty more run-ins before the trip ended.

The horn did not work as intended. A few days later, in the middle of the night while all of us slept, the horn whistle bellowed without prompting, waking all of us up from a restful sleep. It is an understatement to say I was annoyed. I disconnected the power cord and never used that horn again. The best way to avoid dog encounters is to pedal faster than they can run. Dogs tend to go for the ankles and the rotating pedals. My first instinct was always to pedal faster; the second, to yell. Shouting "Go Home!" worked most of the time. The combination of pedaling fast and yelling loudly worked the best. I was not comfortable with using the kick method. I was afraid I might forget to release my shoe from the cleat, lose my balance, and fall over. Several days earlier in California, a dog had attacked Gary as he entered the interstate from the on-ramp. The dog bit through one of his panniers. He was not injured, but that situation made it clear the stories about aggressive dogs were real.

The biggest disappointment on this day was crossing the Rio Grande. I had imagined an enormously wide, fast-flowing river, for some reason. I liken it to meeting a larger-than-life actor who turns out to be much different than how they appear on the screen. I would not have known I was crossing the Rio Grande if not for the "Rio Grande" sign next to the bridge. (Beginning on this day, for several hundred miles, I rode parallel to the Rio Grande. Except for isolated locations, the river was bone-dry.)

About five miles after crossing the Rio Grande, I entered Hatch, New Mexico. Several of us arrived in Hatch about ten that morning. Sparky's Restaurant, famous for its chili burgers, opened at ten-thirty.

Joel, Doug, Tom, and I decided to wait around for a super-early lunch (some might say a second breakfast). People queued up outside the entrance beginning at about ten-fifteen, waiting for the store to open. It was worth the wait. The burger and fries tasted great.

The last thirty miles before reaching Las Cruces were extremely challenging. The oppressively constant headwinds tested my mental fortitude. At one point, riding downhill, I purposely stopped pedaling. My forward momentum halted. I mustered the intestinal drive to press on, but the energy needed to keep forward movement far exceeded that of any other day. I stopped a few times and checked to see if something was wrong with my bike. I worked so hard just to progress a tenth of a mile. To pass the time and keep my mind occupied, I created fictitious villains whose job was to make my life miserable. It went like this: hills, headwinds, heat, and humidity all try to outdo each other. The four H's compete for the title of "Most difficult to ride through." Never wanting to be outdone, just when one H is the most challenging, another one steps in and says, "Not so fast!" This was one of the many head games I played to fill time.

Leading up to the ride and before leaving San Diego, I thought the journey would be a combination of physical and mental challenges. For the first few days, the physical aspect was equal to the mental. The further I rode, the easier the physical part became. I remember riding alongside Wally the day we left Brawley in the California desert and telling him I thought the mental facet of the ride was more difficult. Wally agreed and added, "I want to enjoy the ride, not just finish it." I valued his perspective, knowing three coast-to-coast rides contributed to his collection of ultra-distance cycling adventures.

Riding coast to coast is simply the sum of individual fifty-mile-plus rides on consecutive days. Nothing more. Thinking about the ride this way lessened the feeling of its being an insurmountable task. The weather created the most significant difficulties in the middle part of the ride, especially in Texas, when torrential rains flooded many parts of the state in October 2018. And then, toward the end of the journey, when I could taste the finish, self-doubt entered my mind. I prayed my bike would not fail me, feared my knees would give out, and wondered when the proverbial shoe would drop. The daily grind, requisite grit, and dealing with constant mental gymnastics far outweighed the physical requirements.

REFLECTION

Riding alone east of Mesilla, New Mexico, on State Route 28 en route to El Paso, gave me much time to think and reflect, and so I did.

I was fortunate to be raised in a fantastic family, and now I am blessed to be with my wife and three children, whom I adore. I am determined to live each day to the fullest, to continue pushing myself to the limit, out of my comfort zone. I'm no longer willing to settle for anything other than happiness. My priorities grew more explicit as I made my way across the country. My pessimistic outlook started to fade away, and the important things grew much clearer.

For most of my life, I was a positive person, a friendly person. I chose to be that person. For the past few years, I had found myself looking at things in a much more cynical way. Perhaps it was because of the depression. My family is incredible—parents, four brothers, sisters-in-law, aunts, uncles, nieces, nephews, cousins are all remarkably close. My mom and dad did everything for their five boys.

With five boys in the house, you can imagine that sports were a significant part of our family upbringing. "Go outside and play!" Mom would implore after family dinners or when we were watching too much TV. It was easy to rally friends for a competitive neighborhood basketball or football game. My brothers played organized sports— baseball, basketball, and football. Like many young boys, I dreamed of becoming a professional basketball player. There are many fond memories from my childhood. I worked hard as a youngster. When other kids in the neighborhood were up to no good, I was the one running stairs at the high school football stadium (at night, so no one would see me).

I am so thankful my parents persuaded me to pursue my college education. I worked my tail off and earned a starting spot on the college basketball team in my sophomore through senior years. In 1983, my team, the Susquehanna University Crusaders, took the eventual national champion University of Scranton to overtime and lost a heartbreaking game by six points. My Crusaders earned a trip to the Division III March Madness Tournament in 1984, my senior year. In the regional tournament semifinal game, we crushed our opponent, Franklin & Marshall College, only to fall to Montclair State University in the regional finals. But it did not matter; I was a proud member of a Sweet 16 basketball team.

After college, I entered the United States Army, commissioned as a 2nd lieutenant through my college ROTC program. Military service was an adventure. I played on two post-championship basketball teams (5th Mechanized Infantry Division—the Red Diamond or Red Devils Division) at Fort Polk, Louisiana, and the 2nd Infantry Division (Second to None Division—the Indianhead patch is one of the most recognized unit emblems in the United States Army)[14] at Camp Stanley, Korea. I traveled the world and met incredible people along the way. I left the Army in 1991 and began a rewarding seventeen-year career with Pfizer Pharmaceuticals, selling prescription medications to physicians.

On December 8, 2006, when I learned I'd lost my job during one of the many company reorganizations at Pfizer, my view of work changed. The news of losing my job after seventeen years with Pfizer hit me hard. I was disappointed and shocked. The severance package included an extension of employment until May 2007, and we were encouraged to consider work at other positions within the company. A competitive interview would be part of the rehire process. I did not want to leave Pfizer, so I applied for a couple of openings in different business units. I flew to New York to interview for a job. It felt odd to be interviewing for a position with the same company where I'd worked hard for seventeen

---

14 2ida.org.patch

years. My confidence waned. I questioned whether I wanted to continue my career in the pharmaceutical business.

A friend suggested I look at his firm, a construction company. I knew little about construction, but my friend convinced me it would be a wonderful place to work. I was open to a career change. On the way home, after going on a field ride to see a sales professional in action, I realized that selling construction tools was not my passion. I called the hiring manager and passed on the opportunity. I then took the step of reapplying to join the military. Kelley was not keen on the idea because we had three young kids at home (Tara was fourteen, Jaclyn ten, and Brian, two).

Since the terrorist bombing on September 11, 2001, I had reconnected with my Army past and felt there was more I could do to serve my country. I was eager to explore rejoining the Army, since I did not have a job. I found all my Army records, including my DD 214 (discharge from active duty), sent the necessary paperwork to the right place, and waited for a response from the Department of Defense. It hit me hard when I found out the Army did not need my services. I could not believe it. I was in great shape and had skills that could be used right away, but I was forty-five years old and far past my prime.

I was in a funk, and for the first time in my life, I felt inadequate. I broke down in front of Kelley, not knowing what my future held. I was not well. I could not sleep. I had constant ringing in my ears. I was freaked out about paying the mortgage and all the other family bills. I stopped taking part in all activities, including playing pickup and men's league basketball. My parents saw firsthand that I was not well when we visited them in spring of 2007, and they became concerned. In what I can only describe as catatonia, I stared at the walls of my office and said nothing for hours, days on end. I was confused about why this was happening to me and stunned by the swiftness of my downward spiral.

Tara, my eldest daughter, was entering the tenth grade. Jaclyn was entering sixth grade, and Brian was two years old. We had a beautiful home with a big mortgage. Cleveland was not exactly the hub of pharmaceutical activity, so finding a decent job would be challenging. I was not mentally prepared to put my best foot forward at that time. Even so, I continued looking for work. It took me a while to realize I needed help. Kelley and my eldest brother, Tim, convinced me to see a doctor.

After a few sessions working with a psychiatrist, I continued to struggle. It took several weeks for the medication to kick in and symptoms to improve, but I continued to push forward as best I could. Even though the days were difficult to manage, I found an exciting job opportunity in New Jersey through perseverance and good old-fashioned networking. I was extremely relieved. But something was still not right. I continued to have difficulty sleeping, many nights only getting three or four hours of sound sleep.

In May 2007, I started my new job with Ferring Pharmaceuticals. Kelley and the kids joined me in New Jersey for the start of school in September. I decided to stop taking the medication without consulting a physician. I felt better about myself, but I carried the knowledge that I was prone to depression deep down. It made sense to take a job in New Jersey; should I ever get downsized again, at least I lived in the pharmaceutical hub, so in the future, opportunities would be plentiful.

So in March 2018, when I received the news that I had lost my job with Ferring, I thought I was better equipped to deal with the situation this time. I had a great network. I got along with my colleagues and performed well in all my jobs. But there lay the problem: I considered work just that—a job. Nothing more. I found myself wondering why it was taking so long to get to retirement. I was not a happy person. I am sure friends and family could not tell. But deep down, it just was not me.

But since I'd committed to going on this bike ride, something had changed. Here I was about to cross the Texas border on my way to El Paso, close to Fort Bliss, where I started my journey into adulthood outside the comfort of my hometown in South Central Pennsylvania. The adventure I began thirty-four years ago serving in the US Army was now coming full circle as I gazed up at the Franklin Mountains in the distance, pedaling to a hostel in downtown El Paso.

For 106 miles, between Caballo, New Mexico, and El Paso, Texas, I rode parallel to the Rio Grande. Maximum water flow takes place between April and October; however, much of the riverbed I rode by was dry. The Rio Grande, extending for 1,885 miles, is the fifth longest river system in the United States and establishes part of the Mexico/United States boundary. It is sometimes referred to as the "Forgotten River" to raise awareness of deteriorated conditions along a two-hundred-mile stretch from El Paso to the Rio Conchos in the Mexican state of Chihuahua.[15]

I rode by the Rio Grande winery, a cotton field in La Mesa, and a single lonely and majestic-looking Arabian horse in Chamberino, New Mexico. I rode by Stahmanns Pecans, a pecan farm that is reportedly one of the world's most extensive groves. But the most peculiar sighting occurred shortly after I crossed the Texas border.

Tom and I were about to begin riding down a dirt bike trail that ran parallel to Highway 20 near Canutillo, Texas. It was surrounded by a sea of brown dirt, gravel, and ankle-high sagebrush. Suddenly, a fluffy white bunny with large, pink-lined ears appeared, startling me. I said, "Tom, the killer rabbit in Monty Python!" The iconic scene played out in my head of the killer rabbit leaping to decapitate one of the knights:

Other knights attack, only to be incapacitated. Then, realizing the rabbit is too much to handle, one of the knights panics and shouts, "Run away!" The remaining knights debate whether running away is a good idea. Eventually, they decide on using the Holy Hand Grenade to defeat the killer rabbit. The knights are then free to continue their campaign.[16]

The bunny hopped toward us, paused, then hopped again, getting closer. Finally, it turned and hopped away from us, disappearing into the sagebrush. Seeing a fluffy white bunny in the desert, alone, just seemed so odd. A brown bunny, okay, but not a white bunny. It did not

---

15 Americanrivers.org
16 Montypythonandtheholygrail.com

belong, it was out of place. And yes, I did imagine the bunny jumping up to bite my head off!

The United States is enormous; at four million square miles, it is one of the world's top five countries by total area.[17] But the mind is a powerful tool; I shrank the country down into much smaller chunks, to the point where, after crossing the Texas border, I thought to myself, "Once I get through Texas, I've got a straight shot to St. Augustine. Piece of cake." Before this ride, I could not imagine riding across a single state, let alone the United States, but now it just did not seem all that daunting anymore.

Each of the seven map sections that make up the Southern Tier is between four hundred and five hundred miles. Completing one section is a big deal. Each time I finished one, I placed that map in the bottom of my right rear pannier, my go-to pannier for items I did not use often. I followed this routine to help me remain positive, another mind game that I found extremely helpful. I set different goals for myself each day. Each goal completed meant I was that many miles closer to finishing. I did anything I could to stay focused on the task at hand, the next ten miles, anything to distract me from thinking about St. Augustine and the number 3,100. I had used similar mental techniques effectively in the military quite often.

I placed a picture of an airplane, with 352 steps leading to the plane's entrance, over my bed in the bachelor officer quarters at Camp Stanley and the Quonset hut at Camp Stanton, where I lived while serving in Korea (my tour in Korea was one year). The day I arrived in Korea, and for the next 351 days, I darkened one step at the end of each day. Slowly but surely, the darkened path got closer to the plane entrance. After a two-week field training exercise, I would darken in fourteen steps at one time. That task was ripe with exuberance. I used a similar technique in ranger school. On the inside of my ranger hat, I used a pen to mark the end of a day. It took me eighty-eight days to complete Ranger School.

---

17 www.worldatlas.com/articles/the-largest

I took one day at a time, so each successful day was one day closer to graduation. The way I saw it, the map sections of my bike tour served the same purpose as the airplane and the ranger hat.

Most things are genuinely bigger in Texas, but not everything. This became clear when I realized I had missed the "Welcome to Texas" sign. After realizing I'd crossed into Texas without seeing a border sign, I at once thought about forming a plan B. One of my goals was to take a picture at every state border-crossing sign. I executed plan B by tracking down the first vehicle I saw with a Texas license plate. I needed proof. I approached a lady standing outside her car at a gas station. I explained my dilemma. "Hi, I'm riding my bike across the country. I wanted to take a picture next to the Texas border sign," I said with a wide smile. "But the road I entered Texas on did not have a Texas border sign," I added, somewhat sheepishly. Stella graciously agreed to take my picture next to her car and license plate. If she thought I was a bit odd with such a request, I could not tell. I continued to my destination in downtown El Paso.

As I approached the El Paso city limits, I looked up to the magnificent Franklin Mountains. The mountains brought back memories of 1984 when I was stationed at Fort Bliss, Texas. One night I crashed a fraternity party at the University of Texas at El Paso (UTEP) on the west side of the Franklin Mountains (Fort Bliss is on the east side of the Franklin Mountains). I was a brand-new 2nd lieutenant, only out of college about three months, ready to party with the students. I remember driving there with a couple of Army friends. I walked through the front door and joined the crowd. But I felt so out of place. I looked around, and no one noticed us. It was as if we were invisible. I had a military-style high and tight haircut, not a common look for the students. I do not remember how we found out about the party, nor do I remember how we found its location. All I remember is feeling completely out of place. I had already moved on from frat parties, and it was time to find different weekend activities.

Before checking into the Gardner Hotel and Hostel on Franklin Avenue in downtown El Paso, I stopped at a Starbucks outside of El Paso to connect with my wife about my son's football game. I was fortunate to be able to see highlights on the Hudl app. I passed the time on my bike by visualizing Brian's specific plays—catching a pass, intercepting a ball, or tackling someone. I grabbed onto a highlight and replayed the same play in my mind, over and over. Another technique to help me stay focused.

My sleeping problems had arisen from my mind continually replaying situations at work that I detested. It was like a show reel that kept rewinding. Interactions played out in my head nonstop, to the point where I woke up dreading the day ahead, expecting that a comparable situation awaited me at the office. Now, I grabbed onto the good memories, no longer incessantly focused on negative thoughts. They played out in my mind until I thought of another wonderful memory, which then replaced it, and the cycle continued. Like the joy and happiness in Jaclyn when she shares her zeal for helping people see their natural beauty. And the August day in 2010 when Kelley and I dropped Tara off at High Point University to kick-start her college experience. It hit me that our eldest had grown into such a wonderful young independent person ready to search for her life's passion.

Positive memories of specific events dominated my thinking. After putting my head on the pillow, I would grab onto a positive memory, and before I knew it, I was waking up to the start of a new day.

When I was growing up, my mom and dad always found a way to attend my sporting events. I did my best to attend my two daughters' high school basketball games. Not being able to see Brian's games in person and being separated from my family for an extended time motivated me to keep pushing to St. Augustine.

El Paso did not look familiar to me at all. It was not how I remembered it. The city and the surrounding area have changed dramatically since 1984. Or maybe, because of time, my memory faded. Regardless, when I rode by the "Leaving El Paso" sign, I shook my head, wondering at how different the areas were from when I lived there in 1984.

At the hostel in El Paso we reunited with Deb, Gary, and Klaus, the three group members who'd left us in Palo Verde, California. We celebrated the reunion at a downtown El Paso restaurant. I was thrilled that ten cyclists now shared responsibility for carrying the group gear, rather than seven. I did not weigh my bike after leaving San Diego, but it weighed close to one hundred pounds for the six hundred miles between Palo Verde, California, and El Paso, Texas. Next, we would be riding through the entire state of Texas, one third of the whole Southern Tier route. California, Arizona, and New Mexico were in the rearview mirror. It would be three weeks before we crossed into Louisiana.

October 8 – El Paso to Fort Hancock (55 miles)

The group dealt with a little drama before leaving El Paso. First, Klaus woke up to a flat tire. A minor inconvenience, but an inconvenience nonetheless. The bigger problem was a missing cell phone! Out of the blue, Joel yelled, "I can't find my iPhone!"

At first we did not panic, but then Joel explained that he used his iPhone to navigate; it was his only means of steering across the country properly. He had not brought paper maps and did not own a separate GPS device. His connection to the outside world was gone. Without paper maps, a GPS device, or access to his iPhone, he could be led astray without the benefit of technology to guide dozens of decisions each day. We all stopped what we were doing and began an exhaustive search, retracing our tracks from the night before. Someone in the group drew our attention to a seedy-looking truck on the opposite side of Franklin Avenue. We started asking each other if anyone had spotted strangers in the hostel lobby or outside on the street. Initially, we all thought Joel had misplaced it, but then our collective thoughts focused on the truck across the street, looking for human activity. It was early in the morning, before seven. Not a soul was outside that we could see. About fifteen minutes had passed when suddenly Joel said, "Here it is!" We were all relieved. The days on the saddle had started to take a toll on all of us.

Joel apologized and said he needed to get more sleep so he could process situations more clearly.

I felt anxious and, at the same time, excited about riding through Texas. I wanted to ride on a wide-open, never-ending Texas road. I envisioned myself in the middle of the desert, sand blowing, storms approaching, wondering what I would do. Could I manage the stress?

The rain started to fall shortly after we left El Paso's city limits. The sky was grey and gloomy. I saw blue sky far to the east, trying to peek through the cloud cover. I picked up my pace and tried to pedal to the sunshine. It seemed to me the blue sky stood still, never appearing to move closer to where I was. My windbreaker kept me dry and warm while the bike fenders blocked most of the rain and dirt from spraying onto my legs and backside. I pedaled fast to our destination, a church in Fort Hancock, Texas. I'd decided to install fenders about a week before I left for San Diego. I was one of only three in the group to ride with fenders. I wanted to avoid the gross feeling of tires flinging dirt and water onto my butt and legs when I rode through the storms I knew we would meet on the ride. The fenders worked like a charm many times over the next several weeks.

I arrived at the community church at about 5:00 p.m. The small brick church building was surrounded by farmland to the west and wide-open Texas plains to the north and east. The local high school was located about a quarter mile south of the church. I chose a location next to the kitchen in the back of the church for my sleeping area, before walking to the Fort Hancock High School gymnasium to shower in the men's locker room.

After dinner and the map meeting, a young boy, one of about a dozen people attending a breast cancer awareness event at the community church, walked to the area where we were gathered and handed each of us a ribbon (October is Breast Cancer Awareness Month). Wally asked the boy what it was like living in the area. The boy told us about his daily routine preparing for school in the morning. He woke up at 3:00 a.m. to tackle his daily chores at the family-owned steer farm. His parents owned sixty head of cattle. The family dogs kept the predators away (mountain lions). After completing his morning chores, he went to school. After school, he had more tasks to complete before dinner. All of us were attentive to this young boy sharing a little about life on a ranch in a small southwestern Texas town. I remember thinking about the tremendous cultural gap that existed in different sections of the country. What was most striking about this young middle-school-aged boy was how he confidently interacted with several adult strangers.

A single American flag flew high at the entrance to a ranch halfway between El Paso and Fort Hancock. The American flag caught my attention many more times over the next three weeks.

October 9 – Fort Hancock to Van Horn (75 miles)

We woke up to a pleasant morning after a nasty storm moved through Fort Hancock the night before. At about 2:00 a.m. I was woken up by the snorting and rattling sounds of two group members sawing logs. My earplugs barely blunted the annoying sound. I moved my air mattress and sleeping bag into the kitchen area and lay down on the narrow path connecting the back end of the kitchen to the door leading to the shared area where everyone else slept. In the morning, when we all sat around eating breakfast, preparing to leave the church, Joyce spoke up, saying, "From now on, we are going to assign sleeping locations. The snorers sleep in one area. Everyone else somewhere far away!" She said it half-jokingly, but honestly, no one got a good night's sleep with all that racket going on in such a confined area (except me!).

Blue sky above, cloud cover much further east, and a nice tailwind propelled me when I started cycling away from the church. I did not see a single vehicle for hours. A roadrunner darted out in front of me on a quiet country road—a little excitement on an otherwise uneventful morning. *Beep! Beep!*

The route directed us back onto Interstate 10 for a few miles. I did not want to ride on the interstate again. But I ground it out, focusing my attention on the road shoulders to avoid debris. At the crest of one mountain climb, I looked up and saw a sign that read "Entering the Central Standard Time Zone." *How cool is that!* I thought. I was making progress. It would have been so easy to forget about everything else, to only focus on arriving at the next destination. Several in the group did just that. But why take that approach? To me, that would have been a missed opportunity. I wanted to experience local communities, interact with people, and see how others lived in flyover country. For me, it would have been mundane to simply ride to the next destination, set up camp, and repeat until the finish.

Joel and I arrived in Sierra Blanca at about the same time. Sierra Blanca is the east/west connection point of the second transcontinental rail line. I did not remember learning about it in school. It's like coming in second place in the one-hundred-meter dash. No one knows anything about second-place finishers. Joel, our resident weatherman and retired railroad worker, was delighted to ride through Sierra Blanca. Not one to take many pictures, Joel asked me to take a picture of him next to the rail car. I obliged. I think my dad would enjoy visiting Sierra Blanca. He collected trains when he was a kid growing up in Massachusetts. The border town of Sierra Blanca resembles a ghost town, with the minor exception of an open gas station and a Subway shop. A weathered and abandoned 1950s theater, a weeded-over truck stop, and the boarded-up windows of a once-thriving Chuck Wagon Café were reminders of a better past. It is also notorious for drug trafficking. I did not see anything nefarious during my thirty-minute visit.

By the time I entered Texas, I was no longer waking up with the feeling that I had to pinch myself. I had moved beyond the surreal and embraced the reality of my situation. The confluence of events—injuring my foot, losing my job, being concerned about my mental well-being, and struggling to figure out my future—somehow all led to an internal drive that set the course for my ride across the country. Now I laser-focused on meeting the challenge head-on every day.

October 10 – Van Horn to Marfa (74 miles)

It was a perfect morning when I left for Marfa, Texas. I woke up at the Van Horn campground after a great sleep under the stars. I started riding at seven-thirty, the best time of the day to ride, when the motionless, soundless, brown, barren desert comes alive, the dawn of a sunshine-filled new day. The morning breeze was supplying the perfect balance to the rising sun and the realization that the battle against nature would arrive within hours. On this day, I planned for a seventy-four-mile ride without services between Van Horn and Marfa, a stressful scenario. As the early morning turned to late morning, winds picked up, and for the better part of fifty miles, I dealt with relentless crosswinds and headwinds. Highway 90 runs parallel to the Union Pacific Railroad track. On main lines (principal corridors of the rail system from which branch lines are connected and which refer to a link between towns), which this is, grades are 1 percent or less. A grade steeper than 2 percent is rare. The expected total climb of 1,200 feet for the seventy-four-mile segment is minimal. Yet the ride took a toll on me both physically and mentally.

Several days earlier, Doug had suggested I increase pedaling speed, or revolutions-per-minute (RPM) cadence. The more experienced riders averaged eighty-five to ninety RPMs. I averaged between fifty-five and sixty-five RPMs. The theory is that at a higher RPM, the body works more efficiently; the legs do not work as hard, and knee pain lessens. It sounded like a good thing for me to try, so I did. But when I rode at the higher RPM, I did not feel like I was riding at an optimal speed. I accepted Doug's input and tried to adjust, but it didn't work for me, so I resumed at my own pace.

But on this day, cycling to Marfa along Highway 90, I experienced the single most challenging fifty-mile segment on my trek across the country—a joint mental and physical challenge like no other. I looked toward the horizon on Highway 90 and cycled hard to reach the top of a hill, only to be deflated when I realized the road continued with no end in sight. I rode to phantom crests all day! It was brutal to my psyche. The road never ended, and the headwinds took a toll on me.

I tried to take my mind off the challenging headwinds. I thought about what it would be like to live in this area. I grabbed onto anything that could help occupy my mind. A horse, cow, house, or flagpole with an American or Texas flag flying high kept my attention, enabling me to focus on what might be next. A lone tree in the desert stood out like a sore thumb. On occasion, a train passed, displaying the American flag with the message "Building America" on the locomotive's side. I rode by Ryan Ranch, a 35,000-acre ranch surrounded by the Davis, Chinati, and Sierra Vieja mountain ranges. The 1956 movie *Giant*, starring Rock Hudson, James Dean, and Elizabeth Taylor, was filmed on Ryan Ranch. The name of the ranch caught my attention because my nephew's name is Ryan. I sent a picture of the ranch sign to my brother and added, "I didn't know Ryan owned a ranch in Texas." Several miles later, riding on the same Highway 90, I passed a second sign for Ryan's Ranch. Expansive ranches go on for miles. And as big as Ryan Ranch is, nothing compares to the largest ranch in Texas (by acreage): 825,000-acre King Ranch, an area larger than the state of Rhode Island.[18] Yes, Texas is a big state.

Around noon and thirty miles west of Marfa, I got a glimpse of a structure about one quarter mile in front of me. It was a solitary, uninhabited display structure built into the desert floor called "Prada Marfa." This permanent sculptural art installation was like a monument. The fifteen-foot-long, ten-foot-high rectangular building was a fake Prada purse store, built in 2005 by a Berlin-based art team. It was surrounded by a protective fence, with a small gravel area in front and a low-profile sign describing the history of the display. It stood out, incongruous with the desert landscape. The bizarre roadside attraction is classified as a museum by the Texas Department of Transportation. It is constructed

---

18 Kingranch.com

of a material that will eventually disintegrate and blend right back into the desert floor.[19]

A group of five young adults traveling from Brooklyn to California stopped to check out the unusual structure while I was standing there. They were originally from the Ukraine and Russia. One of the young ladies responded, "Starting a new life," when I asked why they were traveling to California.

This was exactly how I had imagined my ride through Texas. The day did not disappoint, and I knew there would be more like it in the days ahead.

When driving long distances in a vehicle, we tend to stop periodically for food or to fill the gas tank. Hundreds of miles pass between stops. Much of America stays invisible. The surrounding landscape becomes uninteresting, and senses are dulled. A person's focus is on getting from one destination to the next. Traveling on a bicycle is an entirely different story. Small towns become a sought-after destination. The succeeding convenience store becomes the next milestone. A city in the rearview mirror means you're one more town closer to St. Augustine. Visiting small-town America and meeting thought-provoking people brought my ride to life.

October 11 – Marfa (Rest Day)

I woke up in Marfa to a pleasant sunrise. I stood up outside my tent and looked around at all the different lodging options available to El Cosmico hotel guests: Cosmic Kasita trailers, yurts, tepees, safari tents, and my favorite, self-camping. In 2007 Marfa hosted its first music festival. Thousands of attendees camped at the El Cosmico campsite. In 2009, the El Cosmico owners turned the site into what they called a hotel but what was, in actuality, a very eclectic and expansive campsite. Year after year, thousands descend on Marfa and the El Cosmico hotel

---

19 www.inspiredimperfection.com/adventures/prada-marfa

for a Festival of Music + Love. The atmosphere is relaxed, laid-back, a place to experience *manana* (literal meaning: procrastination). There was a good natural vibe given off by the people I met and the places I visited walking through the eighteen-acre campsite and the streets in downtown Marfa. It's a perfect city for people who embrace the philosophy "There's always a reason to wait until tomorrow" or "Why do something today if it can wait until tomorrow?"[20] Think Woodstock, and the picture becomes clear. I truly realized I was far from home when I saw the "Clothing Optional" sign next to the hot tubs, which were exposed to anyone walking by.

On October 21, 2018, American book author, chef, and TV personality Anthony Bourdain featured Marfa in a television series called *Parts Unknown*, where he highlighted the Lost Horse Saloon on East San Antonio Street in the heart of downtown Marfa, about eight tenths of a mile from the El Cosmico. He picked the proper town to explore Southwestern US culture and cuisine. Marfa is the perfect location for a *Parts Unknown* episode. It's extremely remote, a hidden gem, and not many people I know have heard about it. I did not visit the saloon. I only learned the details of Bourdain's visit to Marfa after I left town.

In the center of town, sticking out like a sore thumb, sat the Presidio County Courthouse. It is a multilevel building housing individual office space and an old-style courtroom on the top floor. Wooden benches face the judge's chair and witness stand. It is a tiny and intimate courtroom. I imagined seeing Gregory Peck in *To Kill a Mockingbird* arguing his case to defend Tom Robinson in front of a packed room of spectators. Later that day, walking through town, I was disappointed when I saw a "Closed" sign next to Quintana's Barber Shop on the main street. A few hours later, when I walked back to the El Cosmico after eating at Dairy Queen, I spotted something interesting down a side road. Another barbershop, aptly named "Barber Shop," was open! "Hi, I'm Larry. Are you open for a haircut?" I asked upon entering the single door in

---

20 www.elcosmico.com

the front of the small ranch building resembling a shanty. Instead of a traditional spinning barber pole attached to the front of the building indicating the shop being open for business, a four-foot cylindrical post painted red, white, and blue was set upright in the ground on the front grassy area.

Abe, the barber, welcomed me and pointed for me to take a seat in the only chair. We exchanged pleasantries, he let me know he was a retired sheriff from Marfa, and then our conversation transitioned to my military service. "Really!?" I could not believe it when he told me he had barbered at Fort Bliss, Texas, in 1984. The same year I attended Officer Basic school, Abe worked as a barber on the base. What a coincidence. We tried unsuccessfully to remember specific details about our time at Fort Bliss but concluded nonetheless that there was a chance Abe had given me a haircut thirty-four years ago. I took a picture of Abe, the retired sheriff, town barber, and Southwest Texas cowboy, standing in front of his shop, and chalked up meeting Abe as another memorable encounter on my incredible journey across the country.

I have always enjoyed visiting barbershops, but I never knew the history of the pole. The barber pole is a universally recognized symbol for barbering and can be traced back to the Middle Ages. According to an article about the pole's history, bloodletting inspired the red and white stripes. The barber pole symbolizes a stick that a patient squeezed to make veins in the arm stand out more prominently for the procedure. Patients gripped the post during an operation to encourage blood flow. Red stands for blood, and white stands for bandages used to stop bleeding. Blue stands for patriotism and a nod to our nation's flag. (In Europe, poles are red and white only, and in America, they are red, white, and blue.)[21]

I took advantage of the rest day in Marfa. I spent a lazy day walking down the main street, peeking inside stores, and reading historical markers—everyday activities when I visited a new place on vacation. I stopped in front of the Marfa Opera House to read about the theater's

---

21 www.rd.com/article/barber-pole-history

history. It was built in 1905. At the time, it was the only theater between El Paso and San Antonio, a 550-mile stretch. It was a gathering place for dancing, grand balls, concerts, meetings, plays, banquets, vaudeville shows, silent films, and bingo.[22] But my visit to Marfa was not the type of vacation where I spent money buying trinkets to take home to the kids. I was not about to willingly add any more weight to my bike. (Before leaving for San Diego, my friend Gino asked if I could bring home a shot glass from every state I rode through. The answer was an emphatic NO!)

The combination of cowboys, artists, blue-collar workers, and elites all living in an area equal to less than two square miles did not make a lot of sense to me, especially in the rough-and-tumble isolation of the Southwest Texas desert. When I stumbled upon the Prada store, I knew visiting Marfa would be a unique experience. I was not disappointed. Marfa is a town where I met interesting people and saw cool things. It is also a town in which cycling through is the best way to appreciate its nuances.

October 12 – Marfa to Marathon (57 miles)

I rode through a lot of cloud cover and high humidity the morning I left Marfa. From the top of the courthouse the day before, I had seen clouds covering part of a mountain east of Marfa. As I rode east, the cloud cover lifted, leading to a full view of an attention-grabbing image. The transition from cloudy to clear happened in the blink of an eye—the sky cleared, and the clear mountain view unfolded almost instantly.

About seven miles east of Marfa, I stopped at a viewing area to read about the mystery of the Marfa Lights. A detailed summary describing the mystery was written on a small stone marker next to the parking area. The unusual phenomenon—unexplained flashes of light—has captured people's imagination since the nineteenth century. In the back

---

22 www.marfalivearts.org

of the Marfa Lights observation building, there is a viewing area where people can examine the lights through several telescopes. Explanations for how the lights are seen on clear nights range from scientific to science fiction.[23] During the rest day in Marfa, I heard people talking about their experience seeing the lights. I was not sure what to make of it myself. I spoke to a lady at the El Cosmico who'd visited the lights the night before. She told me she was skeptical before going, but after seeing the lights she believed there was something to the mystery. I concluded I would take the locals' word that it was a cool place to visit. If I visit again, it will be during the Marfa Lights Festival held on Labor Day weekend. Seeing the Marfa Lights would be at the top of the list of things to do. However, on this trip, I settled for reading about the mystifying lights. In hindsight, I wish I had gone. The El Cosmico hotel is about eight miles away from the Marfa Lights viewing area. It is in the middle of the desert. We were traveling on bikes and were exhausted from hours on the saddle each day. I relied on the ACA to arrange the excursions. Had I known the Marfa Lights were such an attraction, I would have found a way to visit on my own.

My body continued to hold up well. I took full advantage of each rest day, walking a lot to stretch my legs. The PMCS I performed twice a day helped to prevent flat tires. Even though the bike performed well, I still stopped by every bicycle shop I saw, if for no other reason than to talk to the employees.

Austin was still several hundred miles away from Alpine, a through town on our trek east, so I decided a tune-up in Alpine was a good idea. The mechanic, a guy named John, trued my tires (used a spoke tool to balance the tires), adjusted the brakes, and lubed the chain. He told me Tank appeared to be in great shape. Even though I was confident about detecting and fixing minor mechanical problems, I still felt the need to rely on a professional. I wanted an independent person's perspective on whether I needed a new chain or new brakes—like a

---

23 Visitmarfa.com/marfa-lights

physician going to another physician for their annual checkup. John had ridden across the country on his bicycle several years before. We had a kindred spirit connection. He did not want to charge me. I gladly handed him twenty dollars cash, thanked him, and left, hoping he was indeed good at his craft.

I had my sights set on Marathon, Texas, for a night of camping under the stars, or so we thought. In the blink of an eye, just east of Alpine, the desert turned green, cattle grazed everywhere; it was an odd feeling. Desert to green in an instant. My senses were acutely aware of the changing environment, a benefit of cycling ten miles per hour rather than sixty in a car.

I arrived at the RV park just west of downtown Marathon at about five in the evening. The group hemmed and hawed before finally settling on pizza for dinner. And when the pizza delivery car pulled up to the campsite, ten adults dropped what they were doing and raced up to the picnic table. We deserved that cheesy, delicious treat.

I looked up to the sky west of the campsite and saw blue with scattered clouds. We followed the weather forecast and knew a storm was heading our way. Except for Klaus, who needed to fix a flat tire from riding over a goathead at the campsite, we all settled in, expecting our time in Marathon to be relaxing and uneventful.

As daylight turned to night, the most ominous-looking clouds dominated the sky to our west. The weather forecast got much worse. Bright sky transformed into dense, turbulent, sinister-looking clouds that loomed over the area due west of our campground, heading directly toward our campsite. Marathon's weather changed instantly; we prepared for a direct hit, seventy-mile-per-hour winds, and hail half an inch in diameter. We quickly moved our bicycles under a covered patio. Bikes are more critical than tents, so we left the tents standing and hoped for the best.

We watched the storm approach from the west. For thirty minutes, ten white-knuckled adults crouched down, eyes focused on the My Radar app on Joel's iPhone, following the storm's path. He gave us the play-by-play. The storm ended up being a dud, at least in Marathon. A little rain and mild winds came through the campground. Thankfully, the storm tracked further east of our location.

After the storm passed, we kept our bicycles under cover but slept in our tents. Travis did not sleep well, hearing the remnants of the storm throughout the night. He snapped a few pictures, including one showing the sky lit up with jagged streaks of lightning blasting to the ground, which he captured at about two o'clock when he peeked outside his tent after tossing and turning throughout the night.

October 13 – Marathon to Sanderson (55 miles)

The following morning the sun shone brightly, and we all set our sights on conquering another day on the saddle in the middle of Southwest Texas. On the outskirts of town, I saw a sign touting an annual Marathon running event called M2M (Marathon to Marathon) held in October. Each year more than five hundred racers compete in this Boston Marathon qualifier. They run in a "dry, cool high desert climate, gradual downhill, spectacular scenery, low traffic, and a downhill to the finish line where you can really pour it on!"[24]

The people of Marathon tout the event as the most significant affair their town puts on. According to the race organizers, "The hardest part is getting there."[25] That is their message to anyone interested in entering the race.

The ride from Marathon, Texas, to Sanderson, Texas, was the single best cycling day for me, period. When I started, I thought the day would be like others. I had ridden for several days on the same road, Highway 90, through small towns in rural West Texas. About two miles into this fifty-five-mile ride, I realized today would be different. The sun was slowly rising. Glorious sunbeams streaked across the sky, to the stars,

---

24 Marathon2marathon.net
25 Marathon2marathon.net

and blinded me as I rode directly toward the horizon. I was surrounded by wilderness, peace, and serenity, with smooth and winding roads for miles. I stopped, attached my GoPro, and for the next fifty-three miles listened to music while sprinting as fast as I could to Sanderson, Texas.

The immediate surprise and excitement of expecting a glorious morning triggered my instinct to yell, so I howled, "Ahhhhhhh!!!!!" for several seconds. I was cruising fast. No one could hear me, see me, or respond to my emotional outburst. I remember thinking how lucky I was to be able to tackle this dream of riding across the country. I thought about my family and how much they meant to me. If there is a heaven on earth for cyclists, it is Highway 90 traveling east between Marathon and Sanderson. John, my hometown friend, had sent me a playlist of songs a few days before I crossed into Texas. The morning calmness made it possible to listen without using earbuds.

"L.A. Freeway" by Guy Clark, "Everybody's Talkin'" by Fred Neil, and Willie Nelson songs repeatedly played for the better part of three hours. The music had a special meaning for me. The night before I left New Jersey, John, his wife, Dana, and their son, Jack, attended the small going-away party hosted by our friends the Griecos. A few months before that party, in February, Kelley and I had attended a celebration of John's brother's life. His brother committed suicide. The all-female band Lez Zeppelin performed at the party in New York City to help raise money for the National Alliance on Mental Illness.

On the night of my going-away party, John shared with me that his brother had ridden his bike coast to coast about a year before his death. That story really struck a nerve in me. So, as I began riding from Marathon to Sanderson, listening to John's music, I found myself thinking about John and his family. The music gave me energy. I felt strong and averaged 18.75 miles per hour for the fifty-five-mile ride from Marathon to Sanderson, a pace that seemed beyond belief, primarily due to the difficulty of carrying close to ninety pounds of weight on my Surly Disc Trucker. I could have continued for three more hours. Tears were flowing. They were happy tears; thoughts of appreciation entered my mind for my wonderful family. On this day, I also rode for my friend John and his family.

For hundreds of miles I rode on Highway 90, which ran parallel to the Union Pacific Railroad line. In the desert, planes, trains, and automobiles are replaced with trains, trucks, and more trains. I saw trains morning and noon and heard them throughout the night. A train whistle blasted for at least fifteen seconds at every town intersection to warn of the train's arrival. No one could sleep through that. In the middle of the desert at 2:00 a.m. when a train rolls through town, the noise is deafening. Most of the trains were double stacked. Joel, our resident railroad expert, contrasted train activity on this ride with train movement in 2008 and 2009 during the recession. He told me the economy must be doing pretty well, evidenced by the constantly running trains. He spoke of seeing countless idle trains in the Northwest during the recession. The large "Building America" logo plastered on the side of train cars did not appear to be false advertising!

Upon reflection, which I often did, I accepted that part of my motivation for taking on this journey was an attempt to forget the challenges in my life that I did not respond well to. I also accepted contrasting explanations, one where I was searching for something unknown to me at the time. Perhaps I would stumble upon a new idea that I could gravitate toward and reinvent myself, setting up a new career that would excite me. At a minimum, I could always tell the story of riding a bike from California to Florida. Some might do their reflecting on a nice walk around the neighborhood. I chose to reflect on a bike ride across the country. While some people might imagine the same thing when looking through the window of a Boeing 737, I acted. I am proud of the fact that I put myself out there.

The night before leaving Sanderson, I ate a delicious bacon cheeseburger and fries at the Ranch House Restaurant, across the street from the Budget Inn. Our waitress was very personable and carried a pistol at her waist. She obliged when I asked to take a picture of her holding her gun. We all behaved. I was unsure what to make of the graphic T-shirt she wore with this inscription on the back: "Once I put his meat in my mouth, I always swallow." Wearing that shirt did not faze her in the least, nor did it faze other restaurant guests sitting close by. I chalked it up to a unique way of life. It was a restaurant experience I do not think I will ever encounter in New Jersey.

October 14 – Sanderson to Seminole Canyon State Park (80 miles)

We'd survived our first week in Texas. Could we survive the second week? The early risers hung a few white lights from a flagpole in the middle of the Budget Inn parking lot to shine on the picnic table where we ate breakfast. Most mornings, the group interacted at breakfast—a little small talk, nothing too heavy, everyone preparing for the day ahead. However, on this morning, before dawn, we ate breakfast mostly in silence. We did not want to wake other guests who were still sleeping. The quiet was disrupted only by the clanking of pots and pans or the rustling of oatmeal containers or breakfast bars being opened. On the road again, along Highway 90 heading east, we all prepared for whatever was in store for us.

The day started like most others. The first few miles were quiet, peaceful, uneventful. The sky was clear, the sun rising over the mountains in the distance. A sense of calm. Rolling hills. Texas was certainly not flat. Do not believe anyone who tells you it is. Riding on a 2 percent grade in the quiet, early morning with no wind is an enjoyable experience. Cycling on the same road in a five-mile-per-hour headwind is extraordinarily challenging. My knee-jerk reaction within one minute of failing to make good progress when cycling directly into a headwind was to look to the sky and yell, "Enough already!!!" Every minor change in riding conditions is amplified tenfold on a bike. When driving in a car with a V6 engine cruising at seventy miles per hour, it's impossible to notice the ground rising underneath the tires. But on a bike, every subtle change in wind or grade is magnified.

About ten that morning before we approached the town of Dryden on Highway 90, I looked up and in the direction of a rising haze in the distance. The nights had been growing longer, allowing temperatures to fall throughout the night, creating conditions ripe for fog. The closer I got, the more precise the picture became. The morning sun rising over the mountains transitioned into a blanket of fog in the blink of an eye. A wall of fog reduced visibility to zero. One minute I saw sunlight. The next pedal rotation, I entered a new world. The sun formed a halo of fog, eventually disappearing entirely. I knew a different world surrounded me, and I knew the only way to get back to the sunny world was on my travel machine, my Surly Disc Trucker. I could not see, and I knew no services existed for a forty-mile stretch between Dryden and Langtry. For the first time since leaving San Diego, I was genuinely concerned for my safety. I turned on all my safety lights and prayed that approaching vehicles could see them. For the next couple of hours, I relied solely on my hearing to warn of oncoming traffic. I rode through the fog for fifteen miles, visibility less than ten feet in all directions. It was a tense cycling experience.

And then, suddenly, I saw blue sky—back to the present.

While we were eating dinner at the Ranch House Restaurant in Sanderson the night before, Joyce had pointed out that Langtry was home to Judge Roy Bean, "the Only Law West of the Pecos," as he called himself. After he died in 1903, Western films and television shows (such as *The Westerner*, a 1940 film starring Gary Cooper, and *Streets of Laredo*, a 1995 TV mini-series starring James Garner) often cast Judge Bean as the Hanging Judge. I was intrigued when Joyce mentioned it to the group and thought I would stop to see the courtroom where Judge Bean had practiced his own brand of law. However, once I saw the blue sky after the tense two-hour ride through fifteen miles of fog, I focused on one thing and one thing only: getting safely to my destination.

I crossed the Pecos River on my way to Seminole Canyon State Park. The bridge over the river was under construction. A temporary blinking construction light managed the single-lane traffic flow across the bridge. The Pecos River is enormous. From my vantage point high above the river, I saw that several hundred feet separated the shorelines. Twenty- to thirty-foot cliffs rose on both sides. Brown water flowed rapidly underneath me, evidence that significant rain had fallen in parts of Texas in the past few days. A crosswind gave me pause. I ignored the signs and started to cross the bridge while the opposite side had the right of way. Luckily for me, the coast remained clear. I made it across safely. The Seminole Canyon State Park is near where the Pecos River flows into the Rio Grande, eventually draining into Amistad National Recreation Area, further east of my location.[26]

Our campsite was three miles off the main route and up winding roads. I was the second to make it to camp. I pitched my tent on the east end of the ridgeline close to Joel, who was the first to arrive. I soaked up the views of the canyons below and the vast surrounding landscape to my east, the direction I would travel the following morning on my way to Del Rio. Reports called for drastically changing weather over the next few days, beginning tonight with rain, winds, and temperatures dropping over forty degrees. We all secured our tents, expecting the worst throughout the night. At about eight o'clock, the rain started to fall. Around midnight the howling winds began, and rain and wind continued into the morning and over the next several days.

I woke up to a muffled roar when the wind collided with my tent. I could hear the distinctive high-pitched sound in the distance as the wind whipped through the west end of the campground. Rain dropped in buckets, and the mercury fell from eighty to forty degrees. At dawn, we huddled around one picnic table, hunched under a small canopy trying to avoid the pounding rain, while reviewing the signs and symptoms of hypothermia.

---

26 www.traveltips.usatoday.com/camping-pecos-river-texas

October 15 – Seminole Canyon State Park to Del Rio (41 miles)

Deb and Gary decided to hitch a ride to Del Rio in a pickup truck. The severe weather would be extremely unpleasant to ride through. There was a greater chance of personal injury due to slippery roads, limited visibility, and relentless cold, wet, pounding rain. The rest of us began our short forty-one-mile trek to Del Rio. After ten miles of riding in the rain and wind, I began to shiver and felt my core body temperature drop. I had not dressed appropriately for the horrible riding conditions. I sweated profusely. Sweat mixed with chilly rain and wind is a dangerous combination. I knew I had to find shelter soon. I rode toward the town of Comstock and prayed something was open.

Surrounded by nature's fury, I was completely isolated on Highway 90, my body cold, hands and feet numb. I was searching for shelter when I spotted a small building about one hundred yards ahead of me. As I approached the Comstock Motel, I became anxious. "Is it open or just another condemned building along the highway?" I asked myself. I stopped, parked my bike underneath a small awning outside, walked up to the small office entrance, and opened the door. Immediately my body temperature rose. The warm air hit me like a ton of bricks. It felt good to be inside. A middle-aged man looked at me without saying a word. I told him I was cold and asked if I could use the dryer. Shortly after, a woman appeared from the back office. They allowed me to use their dryer and gave me access to a vacant room to change my clothes.

The man and woman I met at the front office were a mother and her son who hailed initially from Kentucky. We had a very brief conversation before I took the key and made a beeline for the vacant room. I had one goal in mind: change into dry clothing and properly layer my upper torso attire to safely finish the ride to Del Rio. I wondered how these two people from Kentucky had made it to the middle of Southwest Texas. Maybe they were somehow related to Judge Bean. Judge Bean was originally from Kentucky, and Langtry was about twenty-five miles west of Comstock. Perhaps it was simply chance, but the fact that the judge, mother, and son ended up in this remote section of Southwest Texas seemed oddly coincidental. This would not be the only time the present connected with history on my trip across the country. Clothes now dry, body temperature back to normal, I decided to continue. I took their business card so that I could write a thank-you note to my two trail angels when I returned home.

When I resumed my ride, I had a tailwind, which took the edge off the nasty rain, wind, and cold temperature. I focused one hundred percent on the next milestone, crossing the Amistad Reservoir. The Governor's Landing Bridge fifteen miles northwest of Del Rio spans the Amistad Reservoir, stretching 5,462 feet shoreline to shoreline and rising fifty-sixty feet above the water. When I looked up and saw a single lane each way, a one-foot shoulder full of debris, and a six-inch curb leading to a two-foot-tall side railing, I became anxious. The crosswinds, limited shoulder, and low side barrier were all cause for concern.

Before leaving New Jersey, I did my homework, considering points along the route where I needed to put safety ahead of all else. I had made a mental note of the Governor's Landing Bridge. Pictures I viewed made it seem extremely dangerous. Now that I was here, I couldn't imagine *not* riding my bicycle across. I was determined to finish the entire cross-country ride on the saddle at this point. No shortcuts for me. None! I waited for the right time and then started to pedal. Several minutes later, I made it across without any problem. I stopped and took videos of the surrounding area. The winds howled. I was relieved. I faced the challenge head-on, made it across safely, and thought, there's one less obstacle to confront on my way to St. Augustine.

It was forty-three degrees when I entered Del Rio city limits—thirty-five with the wind chill factor. My Smartwool 100 long-sleeve base layer had managed to help me keep a tolerable body temperature on the thirty-two-mile ride after leaving the Comstock Motel. I was relieved when I arrived at the Motel 6 on Veterans Boulevard and was finally under cover. After a long hot shower, I changed into my green Columbia hiking pants and ActivSkinz 100 SPF lightweight blue long-sleeve shirt, walked to the laundry room carrying everything else I owned, and threw it all into the dryer. The forecast for the next few days was more of the same. Nasty weather! After settling into my motel room, I tallied my total miles. I felt a sense of accomplishment: I was 1,400 miles closer to St. Augustine.

I called Kelley. It was the first time I had talked to her in forty-eight hours, because I did not have cell service. The nasty Texas weather had become national news, so she was not surprised when I told her about my rainy, cold, miserable day on the saddle. The group faced a dilemma. Flooding had caused many roads to close in the area surrounding Del Rio. I told Kelley I did not know the riding plan for the next few days. I asked her to call my folks and let them know I was okay.

I had been very enthusiastic when I entered Surprise, Arizona, west of Phoenix, on my way to Tempe. It was hot and sunny. There was activity all around me. I had a huge feeling of accomplishment. A rest day was ahead and an opportunity to take in what Tempe had to offer. I had vastly different thoughts as I rode up to the Del Rio city limits. It was rainy, cold, and windy, and there were grey skies as far as I could see. I was miserable. My body was wet and cold, and everything I owned was soaked inside and out. Cars sprayed me with water as they drove through the flooded roads. The visual image I'd had of Del Rio, this lovely, quaint small town, did not exist. Perhaps a cozy downtown area was close to the motel, but I did not care to know. The motel was on the busy through street that brought me into town. I wanted to take a warm shower, dry off, and rest my body. That is what I did.

There are bound to be conflicts anytime ten strangers spend an extended time together. The ACA organizes self-contained tours such that camping and cooking outside are the norm. Staying in motels and eating at restaurants is considered a luxury. I enjoyed sleeping in a warm motel bed, just like the rest. And a dinner cooked by someone else at a restaurant was a nice bonus too. But unlike the others, I did not have a strong opinion one way or another about eating at a restaurant or cooking under the stars. I went with the flow. Not everyone agrees with every decision; leaders cannot make everyone happy. To keep costs down, the ACA budgets a reasonable fixed amount per day for food and sleeping accommodations. Several weeks before, in Palo Verde, California, I had sensed friction among some group members, particularly about lodging and eating decisions.

However, I held strong views about completing the ride entirely on a bike. No shortcuts. No bypassing areas because of extreme weather conditions. When I was in my early twenties, my younger brother Dennis and I drove a car across the country from Pennsylvania to San Diego. This time I was cycling across the country, period, end of story.

The afternoon we arrived in Del Rio, Joyce called a meeting in the motel lobby to explain that the planned route for the next day's ride was flooded and impassable. All the options presented to us included renting a vehicle, loading the bikes, and driving around the flooded areas. We then would pick up the sanctioned route again, when and where roads were passable.

Most everyone agreed with the proposed plan. I became very uneasy with the discussion. People react to situations differently, and leaders come in all shapes and styles. I approach everything I do with an inner drive and determination, speaking out when I need to, leading by action, always. I was confronted with one of those situations when I felt it necessary to speak out. I raised my hand to get everyone's attention. All eyes turned to me. I told the group that while I understood everyone's concern about the riding conditions and did not challenge anyone's judgment, I wanted to find an alternate route to continue cycling the following day. I proposed continuing east on Highway 90 toward San Antonio; at some point, I would turn north to connect with the group in a couple of days. I did not want to leave the group, but I was determined to keep pedaling. Going to sleep that night, I tossed and turned, nervous about what lay ahead for me.

October 16 – Del Rio to Uvalde (73 miles)

In the morning, Joyce requested that we all meet at an IHOP (next to the motel) to discuss alternatives. She had found a new route that would enable us to continue cycling to Fredericksburg. The route bypassed flooded roads and eventually reconnected with the primary route. So much rain had fallen the past couple of days in the Texas Hill Country, the direction we were headed, that the ACA canceled a Texas Hill Country bike tour. Fredericksburg and the surrounding hill country had received several inches of rain, making many roads impassable. Doug, Travis, Gary, and Deb decided to rent a car and drive to Austin. Joyce and Klaus rented a car and carpooled to Uvalde, at which point they would continue riding with the group.

Tom, Joel, Wally, and I packed our bikes and began pedaling east to the Days Inn on Main Street in Uvalde, Texas. I was happy to be back on the saddle, riding as part of a group, albeit a smaller one. Everyone respected the others' decisions. We were touring, not racing. Everyone had their reasons for being there, which were shared with the group the night before leaving San Diego. The bond grew stronger between the four of us who continued cycling. We left Del Rio about 10:30 a.m., several hours later than our usual start time. None of us knew what to expect. Busy roads? Flooded roads? Headwinds? We had a motel waiting for us in Uvalde, seventy-three miles to the east along Highway 90. That much we knew.

Cycling was especially challenging due to the cold and wet riding conditions. Traffic picked up the closer we got to San Antonio. I remember thinking, when I saw a sign for San Antonio, that I had made substantial progress crossing the state of Texas. A slight tailwind helped propel us forward.

Once again, I did not dress appropriately for the riding conditions. The moisture-wicking Smartwool sweater did not work as intended; it was designed to draw moisture to the fabric's exterior, making it easier to evaporate. But because I wore rain gear, the sweat could not escape.

My core body temperature dropped. The sweat poured from my body, trapped inside, and made for a very unpleasant ride. But by now, I was used to riding in the rain. I blocked out of my mind the nasty weather and focused on completing ten miles at a time. I thought back to the first week, riding through California, dreading the possibility of cycling in rain and cold. Those nasty conditions were my new reality, and there was nothing I could do about it except to keep pedaling.

Meeting other cyclists on the road turned out to be an almost daily occurrence. About halfway to Uvalde, I spotted a cyclist resting underneath a makeshift shelter across the median. Jordan had started riding from the Bronx in July, heading for his uncle's ranch in New Mexico. He rode south to Florida, then turned west, picking up the Southern Tier route somewhere near St. Augustine. Years before, he had enlisted in the military and served a tour in Afghanistan. The thing that stood out most about Jordan was his choice of equipment. He wore cotton clothing and rode a fully loaded mountain bike fitted with canvas sacks attached to the front and rear racks. Although I questioned Jordan's choice of equipment, he had made tremendous progress, so who was I to judge him?

October 17 – Uvalde to Lost Maples State Natural Area (60 miles)

I left Uvalde early to beat traffic and continued for about twenty miles on Highway 90 before turning north on Highway 127. Not a moment too soon, because traffic increased the closer I got to San Antonio. I felt safe riding on the road shoulders in Texas even though trucks and cars buzzed by, their number increasing exponentially the closer I got to a populated town. I used my rearview mirror continually, checking for vehicles, especially trucks that snuck up behind me without much notice. Vehicles rarely honked. Most of them swerved to the opposite lane and passed when it was safe to do so. Cars and trucks gave me the right of way. A Texas wave always followed.

It was hard to believe, but the weather got worse the further north I rode. We had been riding for one month the morning we left Uvalde. Every day was surprisingly different, each one posing new challenges, but the one pattern that was becoming constant was the rain. I saw high-water mark signs in several areas that were prone to flooding. I entered the small town of Utopia before making my way to our campsite. The rain and nasty weather did not make this place a utopia for me!

The residents of Utopia are immensely proud of their town. Several signs displayed a "Welcome to Utopia" greeting on the road before we entered the small downtown area. Tom and I stopped at the general store in the center of town to rest. Typically, if two of us arrived at a store simultaneously, one of us would stay outside to watch the bikes. We'd already had one incident of theft in San Diego. Doug's sleeping bag was stolen off his bike outside a store when he left it unattended. In Utopia, we concluded the bikes would be safe alone, and both of us entered the store for about a thirty-minute break.

Getting to our campsite inside the Lost Maples State Natural Area was a chore. The office manager told me the primitive camping area was open, but the road to get there remained underwater. It would be the first but not the last time I would have to navigate a significant water obstacle. I strung parachute cord inside the bathroom and hung wet clothing overnight, trying to dry it. Many of my clothes were still wet in the morning due to the high humidity outside and inside the bathroom. The hand dryer did a decent job of removing some of the moisture from my soggy socks.

Texas was in the middle of a multi-day rain event. We pitched our tents in a grassy area next to a covered picnic table. A family in an RV joined us for appetizers. When they started walking back to the RV to settle in for the night, we looked at our tents and then at each other and just shrugged our shoulders, all thinking the same thing: it would be nice to sleep inside their RV tonight! I felt completely removed from civilization inside the Lost Maples State Natural Area campsite. After dinner, I hunkered down inside my tent and went to sleep before eight-thirty—no cell service.

October 18 – Lost Maples State Natural Area to Ingram (42 miles)

Upon exiting the campsite, the morning ride greeted us with a half-mile, 10 percent grade climb, setting the tone for the next fifteen miles: headwinds, rain, cold, and fog. I was disappointed to ride through the Texas Hill Country in such miserable weather. I'd heard so many wonderful things about this area. Cycling enthusiasts come from all over the United States to ride through the hill country. I am sure the scenery is picturesque, but I did not see much of it. The mist, fog, and slight drizzle obstructed most of the views of the surrounding hills.

Joel and I rode at the same pace this day. At the intersection connecting us to Highway 39, we paused for a few minutes to get our bearings straight. The Guadalupe River ran parallel to Highway 39. Two days before, the area had received nine inches of rain in half a day. Parts of Highway 39 were closed due to flooding the day before. We took our chances, and lucky for us the water had subsided in most flood-prone sections of the road.

While I waited to ride through one of several flooded road sections, a man in a pickup truck wearing a cowboy hat drove through the water toward me and stopped to chat. He asked if I wanted to put my bike in the back of his truck and hitch a ride over the flooded road. I thanked him but declined the offer. He acknowledged my decision, and before driving off, he told me, "We all need to help each other." I could not agree more with his sentiment.

I likely would not have been able to ride safely through the raging water currents a day earlier. Soon after the chat with the man in the truck, I arrived in Hunt, Texas, the unofficial halfway point on the Southern Tier route. I walked into the general store and introduced myself to John, the store manager. I slowly walked back and forth between and along the aisles for no reason except to delay the inevitable return to riding in nasty weather. Because I was loitering, he nervously asked if I was looking for anything specific. I responded, "Nothing, just trying to warm up a little." He nodded, and I continued, "Did you know Hunt is the halfway point on the Southern Tier route?" John said he was aware of that and often saw cross-country cyclists stop in his store on their way through town.

I bought a Coke, and a Gatorade for the road, and then sat down between a couple of big rough-looking guys who wore authentic high-crowned, wide-brimmed cowboy hats, a defining piece of attire for American cowboys. They entered the store about one minute before I arrived after exiting their blue Silverado truck, the raised wheel wells and extra-large deep tire treads perfectly matching their ruggedness. One guy sported a full mustache, the other a Fu Manchu mustache; both were reserved and indifferent. They gave me a strange look. I asked how they were doing. I tried to break the ice by saying, "This weather sucks, doesn't it?" and followed up with, "Can you tell me what the roads are like heading east to Ingram?"

It took a couple of minutes, which seemed like an eternity, for them to warm up to me, but eventually we continued a conversation. One guy asked, "How was the road leading into Hunt?"

"Flooded, but passable," I said.

He said I should expect the same conditions between Hunt and Ingram. It was about 12:30 p.m., and the second guy shared, "The sandwiches are really good here."

"I think I will try one," I responded and stood up, walked to the counter in the back of the store, and ordered a cheeseburger and fries. After I finished eating, John took a picture of the two cowboys and me sitting next to each other. We were all smiles. I added three more handshakes to my total on this trek and continued my way.

Klaus's culinary skills took center stage in Ingram, Texas. Joel, Doug, Klaus, and I roomed in one suite at the Hunter House Inn & Suites while Joyce and Wally stayed in a separate suite. Our suite had two bedrooms, one bathroom, a kitchen, and a living room. Several of us watched NFL football (Wally was glued to the tube because his favorite team, the Broncos, were playing). At the same time, Klaus cooked authentic German schnitzel, one of the trip's better meals, with vegetables, salad, warm bread, and apple pie. We took turns using the single washer and dryer in the suite. The night reminded me a lot of my senior year in college, living in an apartment off-campus with three underclassmen. In 1984, my senior year, the night would just be getting started after dinner. In 2018, the day ended abruptly after dinner.

October 19 – Ingram to Fredericksburg (39 miles)

The multi-day weather event was not about to let up anytime soon. It was cloudy, and rain threatened when I started riding about 8:00 a.m. The rain was not forecast to begin until early afternoon, but one mile into my ride, it began to rain in earnest. To make matters worse, Tank started to give me problems. The gears skipped when I shifted. I initially thought the cables needed adjusting, but my hands were too cold to do anything about it. My glasses fogged up terribly; I could not see two feet in front of me. I certainly could not read the GPS. Despite the poor weather conditions, I still enjoyed riding through the Texas Hill Country, meandering through the countryside, watching cows graze in the pastures.

I was in Texas, not Kansas, but *The Wizard of Oz* popped into my mind for some reason. Riding along Rocky Ridge Ranch Road in Kerr County, I thought of Miss Gulch riding a bike down a dirt road, threatening to have Toto put to sleep for biting her, Dorothy chasing behind. Rocky Ridge Ranch Road and Miss Gulch's trail were eerily similar. My mind was free to think. Why certain things popped into my mind when they did, I cannot say. But they did.

I cycled past a long driveway entrance leading to the property of someone named Brian Lane. That caught my attention and got me thinking about how much I missed my family. Further along, a Texas-sized "Kelley's Ranch" sign caught my attention. Both of these instances were reminders of the parallel universe I currently inhabited. Cycling on the road in the middle of Texas removed me from my life back home. I was stepping away and riding into the heart of America, a time that sharpened my thinking and changed my outlook on what was important.

My hotel room was not yet available when I arrived in Fredericksburg. I dropped my bike off for repair at Jack & Adam's Bicycles on Lincoln Street and decided to walk around downtown Main Street. Josh, the shop owner, worked me into his schedule. The rain had stopped by then, but the skies remained grey. I was walking down the road from Lincoln to Main Street, not paying attention to my surroundings, when a truck door swung open directly in front of me. A man stepped out of the truck, and we made eye contact. "Hey, did I see you about twenty miles back?" he asked.

"You're the guy who stopped and asked me and my buddy if we needed help," I replied.

Sure enough, about two hours west of town, on a quiet country road, Errol had stopped when he saw Joel and me, appearing to be lost, huddled around my map, trying to figure out where we were. We were second-guessing each other after taking a left at a Y in the road about half a mile earlier, and he was there to help. We thanked him for stopping but declined his offer to drive us to Fredericksburg. Errol, originally from Zimbabwe, was an avid cyclist and a practicing neuroradiologist in the area. I perked up when he told me what he did for a living. I asked if he knew my brother Dan or a childhood friend, who were both radiologists. His answer was no. (Why wouldn't they know each other? It's a country of only 330 million people.)

I wanted to see as much as possible in the remaining hours of daylight, including the National Museum of the Pacific War in the heart of downtown Fredericksburg. A brick honoring Wally's uncle, who served in the Pacific Theater, was placed on the outside grounds, and next to it a brick honoring his best friend, who died under similar circumstances. Along with these were bricks for many others who perished, victims of atrocities associated with the Bataan Death March. It was a very solemn moment.

Across the street from the museum is the site of Admiral Nimitz's home. He was a significant figure in our nation's history from small-town USA. Unfortunately, the museum closed about fifteen minutes after we arrived. I plan to visit Fredericksburg with Kelley and the kids someday. The history, nightlife, food, and proximity to Austin make Fredericksburg an attractive vacation or cycling destination.

The group ate a dinner of authentic German cuisine at Der Lindenbaum Restaurant on Main Street in downtown Fredericksburg. Klaus was finally able to converse with a waitress in his native language. Downtown Fredericksburg is charming. The main street was full of activity. I heard live music on my walk to the motel after dinner. One band played Eagles hits, and another was playing various country songs. I contemplated entering the bar where the Eagles songs were playing, but decided sleep was more important than entertainment.

October 20 – Fredericksburg to Johnson City (30 miles)

The routes developed by the ACA avoided main roads when possible. I did not study the map before I left Fredericksburg at eight in the morning and was not paying attention when I missed the turn at the edge of town that would have taken me to the primary route through the countryside, a picturesque and less traveled road. About five miles outside of Fredericksburg, it dawned on me that I had missed the turn several miles earlier. My mistake turned out to be a good thing. Before leaving Fredericksburg, I had contemplated whether to ride off-route to tour Lyndon B. Johnson's ranch. I was not sure if I would make it. But the world must have wanted me to see it, as my mistake brought me directly to the LBJ ranch's main entrance.

On the way to the ranch, I passed wineries, cattle, and many American flags flying high and proud. (American and Lone Star State flags flew proudly in almost every town I had ridden through since entering Texas at El Paso, five hundred miles west of Fredericksburg.) For the first time in five days, the clouds broke, the sun peeked out, and rain was not in the forecast. I had become so used to nasty weather by now that I did not care, and in fact, I embraced riding in the rain. I felt that accomplishing a cross-country ride would be tough enough, but completing the journey in dismal weather would give me an even greater sense of satisfaction (it rained twenty-one of the fifty-seven days on the saddle). My mindset shifted from one of "Why so much rain?" to one of "Bring it on!" I could not control the riding conditions. The only thing I could do was react. And the way I reacted would decide the outcome. Attitude played such a critical role in my journey.

I rode my bicycle around the eight-mile loop surrounding LBJ's ranch. Bison and antelope roamed the fields. Hereford cattle sauntered freely, unencumbered by cars (or, in my case, a bicycle). Occasionally I startled a cow, causing it to run away. Several dozen followed behind—a sight reminiscent of wildlife grazing in the plains only to be startled by a loud noise, all running away. I must have looked threatening.

I cycled within five feet of a steer, menacing horns protruding from its head (too short to be a longhorn) and wondered if I was being reckless. I stepped inside the one-room school where LBJ learned to read and write. I spent several minutes at the family cemetery where Lady Bird, LBJ, and many other family members are laid to rest.

Johnson was president during the Vietnam era when there was so much strife in the country. I was young at the time. The United States was struggling with many societal issues, including war and poverty. Racial tensions were also a cause of many problems. My wife has shared stories about seeing the impact of the 1968 race riots in Detroit, where she grew up. Unfortunately, similar issues have bubbled to the surface today, some fifty years later. (As I write this, we are currently amid the COVID-19 pandemic, societal strife, and civil unrest with protests, riots, and looting in many urban areas. Businesses have been destroyed and lives turned upside down. It is tragic.)

Standing over LBJ's final resting place, I thought about the contrast between the upheaval of the 1960s and this day, October 20, 2018. I felt such quiet. LBJ was a larger-than-life figure who led the country through turbulent times. How we all yearn for these turbulent times to subside. I rode by the Texas White House, the airstrip where Air Force One-Half is on display, and parallel to the Pedernales River before finally leaving LBJ's ranch.

A few miles later, I arrived at Johnson City, Texas, our destination for the night. A stretch of nine straight days on the saddle had taken a toll on the group, including me. A rest day in Austin could not come soon enough. I sat with Joyce and Wally at a Dairy Queen across the street from the Hill Country Inn in Johnson City, and we reminisced about our visit to the Pacific War museum. Joyce and Wally both said they planned to relax on our rest day in Austin. I chimed in and added, "I'm looking forward to lightening my load a little, dividing the group gear so Doug and Travis ride with their share!" The extra few pounds carried by only six cyclists had weighed heavily on us the past few days.

October 21 – Johnson City to Austin (50 miles)

We began our trek to Austin at about 7:30 a.m., riding on Highway 2766. The sun rose slowly, surrounded by wispy cloud cover. There was no threat of rain in the forecast. A quiet, tranquil morning began to unfold. While we had ridden through the Texas Hill Country for the past two days, today was the first time I truly enjoyed the experience. The smooth, flat roads transformed into rolling hills right before my eyes. I saw a small speck silhouetted at the top of a prominent Texas hill about half a mile in front of me. That tiny speck was a cyclist in my group. I squinted and realized a second rider was a few feet away from cresting the hill. I shifted gears and began to pedal hard and fast, hoping to generate enough momentum to propel myself to the top of the big hill. The short up-and-down hills compensated for the steep 15 percent grade along Bee Cave Road in the West Lake Hills outskirts of Austin. The phantom hill crests that I'd seen in the western part of Texas were now constant rolling hills resembling a roller coaster ride.

The bike shop owner in Fredericksburg had told us about potential water obstacles that he was confident we would meet the closer we got to Austin. He mentioned sections of the road that were flooded continuously, even after several days of dry weather. I had put that thought aside until, sure enough, I looked down a hill and saw raging water crossing a narrow road.

Fast-moving water flowed. A closer look revealed white foam on both sides of the road. This was a sign that the water flowed over uneven ground, most likely rocks or other natural immovable debris. A short, steep climb followed on the other side of the water. Because the water continuously flowed, we believed the road surface underneath was very slippery, a slimy film that could prove treacherous. Klaus, Tom, Joel, and I were all together at this point. Klaus crossed first. We felt he was the best one to assess the crossing because his tires were thick. He made it across okay. Joel crossed next. As he crossed, the raging water pulled his trailer to the edge, where it almost fell into the rapids. I crossed next. I had just gotten across when my bike swerved to the left. I fell off. My back left pannier came loose. Luckily, I kept control and recovered without falling into the rapids. I pedaled to the top of the hill. We all looked back and waited for Tom to cross. "You've got this, Tom! Stay straight and don't stop pedaling," I said, as Tom prepared to cross the fast-moving water, which he did without any problem. It was an intense few minutes. We were all relieved and glad to have made it across. I was not concerned for my safety; my only reservation had to do with losing equipment if something fell off my bike. The water was moving so fast there would not have been any chance to recover it. That did not happen, so I was relieved. We were fortunate to cross the day we did. It would have been almost impossible two days earlier.

I entered a residential neighborhood about five miles west of Austin. I was surprised by all the hills and the similarities between the suburbs west of Austin and the housing developments in the San Clemente foothills of Southern California, where our family had lived. Many cyclists were riding on this sunny Sunday afternoon. Several looked like legitimate, serious racers. Their legs, torsos, and gear all reminded me of Lance Armstrong (Armstrong grew up in the Dallas area and spent time in Austin). One of them quipped, "Good luck riding with all your gear," as he passed me and I began to climb the steepest hill of the 3,100-mile journey, at least a 20 percent grade. He did not hide his sarcasm very well.

As I began my ascent, I at once realized it was going to be a big challenge. About halfway up the hill, my gears and chain started to skip. I could not continue. I stopped and tried to fix the problem. I could not figure out the problem, so I weaved back and forth for the second half of the climb, avoiding pointing my bike directly up the hill. I finally made it to the top and thought how fortunate I was to be so close to a bike shop in Austin. For the first time, I was concerned that Tank was not up for the challenge of transporting me from the Pacific Ocean to the Atlantic Ocean.

I crossed the Colorado River (for the second time) and rode along the Lance Armstrong Bikeway into the heart of Austin. I weaved in and out of the crowded sections of town. Live music, family gatherings, people tossing Frisbees, a throng of people walking, cycling—the city hummed with activity. Often when I arrived in a small town and walked into a store looking like I did (dirty, sweaty, bike full of gear), people noticed and looked at me strangely, but this was not the case in Austin, where cycling is popular. Even though my bike weighed close to ninety pounds, I blended in well.

I rode through downtown Austin on my way to the Super 8 Motel on Frontage Road close to I-35 on the east side of town. A front desk worker did not allow me to check in, because Joyce held the reservation. Joel and Tom arrived shortly after I did. Doug and Travis had already made it to town. None of us could convince the employee we were all part of the same group. Joyce would not arrive for a couple of hours. We tried to persuade the front desk clerk to allow us to swap out credit cards. No luck. Frustration set in. An hour after we arrived at the motel, a manager changed course, allowing us to check in after realizing we were not taking another group's reservation. This experience tested our patience. It was one of the few times that a motel employee or convenience store worker did not go above and beyond to make us feel welcomed.

I settled into my room, showered, and then rode my bike to Bicycle World on Lamar Boulevard on the south side of Austin. Within a couple of minutes, the mechanic found a problem. I needed a new chain and a new chainring. Two teeth on the small chainring were bent, causing the chain to skip. My inability to use the granny gear had brought about my difficulty in climbing the hills west of Austin. The mechanic assumed the significant torque I put on the pedals while riding at the higher gears had led to the problem. The shop did not have a replacement chainring. If I ordered a new one, it would take at least a day to arrive. The mechanic shaved the teeth, removing the bent section—a short-term fix. I contacted Chet at Whippany Cycle in New Jersey to arrange for shipment of a new chainring to a bike shop in the next-closest town east of Austin. But after assessing the situation, I called Chet and canceled the shipment, deciding instead to continue riding with two shaved teeth on my small chainring. My rationale was that I might not need lower gears because, according to the elevation profiles on the remaining map sections, the most difficult climbing was a thing of the past, now that California, Arizona, and New Mexico were in the rearview mirror.

An old Army friend had driven three hours from Dallas to meet me for a night out in downtown Austin. Carlos and I had not seen each other in nearly twenty years. We ate dinner at a restaurant on the famous 6th Street and reminisced about old times. I had flashbacks of our time together at Fort Ord, California, from 1989 to 1991, where we both served in the same battalion, 2-62 ADA, a unit of the 7th Infantry Division (Light). What great memories! Aside from military service, we shared a love for basketball. After reveille and PT (physical training), we played basketball before morning formation three or four days each week. (At formation at 8:00 a.m. every morning, the battalion first sergeant barks instructions to the troops, signaling the start of the workday). During lunch, we played a few games at the post gym, conveniently located across the street from the battalion HQs. Every Saturday morning and Sunday night, and even some weeknights, we played pickup basketball at the gym on the Presidio of Monterey, home of the Defense Language Institute Foreign Language Center. My first time playing in a 3-on-3 Gus Macker Tournament (a nationwide event for players of various ages and skill levels) was with Carlos in San Jose, California. Downtown San Jose shut down for the event. Hundreds of portable hoops peppered the streets. Teams from all over the country competed to bring home the gold.

After Carlos left the Army, he went to work for Nike in Oregon. At the time, Kelley and I lived in Issaquah, Washington, about three hours north of the Nike headquarters. On one trip to visit Carlos, I entered the Nike gym to play in a pickup basketball game, unwittingly wearing Adidas sneakers. Carlos looked at my shoes and said, "You can't wear Adidas sneakers on the Nike court!" He found a pair of proper Nikes for me to wear. I had dodged a bullet. I do not think I would have been welcomed by other Nike employees wearing Adidas shoes! It was great to see Carlos. Some of my fondest memories of the Army include hanging out with Carlos. (I still wear the Cole Haan dress shoes I bought during a visit to the Nike campus in 1997.)

October 22 – Austin (Rest Day)

My body needed a break. Saddle sores had developed a couple of days earlier, causing a lot of pain on my bottom. (A saddle sore is an irritation of the skin that results from contact with a saddle for too long.) Saddle sores can become showstoppers if they get infected. Saddle sores and knee pain were the two primary concerns I'd had when contemplating my coast-to-coast ride. For novice cyclists, saddle sores are a pervasive problem. I wanted to take care of the issue before it progressed into a nasty infection. I pondered why they developed halfway through my ride rather than earlier, when my body was adjusting to riding several hours a day. I believe the constant rain, sweat, and never-ending seat friction caused the irritation.

I walked to Total Men's Primary Care on Congress Avenue in downtown Austin. The physician's assistant told me my saddle sores did not look infected but prescribed an antibiotic and instructed me to take the pills if the irritation did not improve. I did not take the antibiotic, but from then on, I felt more confident knowing I carried what I needed to stay well.

I walked a lot on rest days. The different exercises and stretching all seemed to create nurturing conditions for the healing of my body. There is so much to see in Austin: the state capitol, the Texas Longhorn football stadium, bars and restaurants on 6th Street, and much more. My day's highlight was when John, another Army friend, drove three hours from Houston to visit with me. John and I met in 1987. We were stationed in Korea, serving together in the 2nd Infantry Division. (I had kept videos that John filmed of my post-basketball team competing against rival teams in the 2nd Infantry Division. My team, 2-61 ADA, won the 2nd Division Championship in 1987. It is fun to watch and listen to John call the game. His voice is very Texas and very distinct.)

I left Korea in March 1988 when my one-year tour ended, and then I began a nine-month temporary assignment at Fort Benning, Georgia. After completing advanced infantry officer school and ranger training, I moved to Salinas, California, and served in the 2-62 ADA of the 7th Infantry Division. Coincidentally, John was stationed at Fort Ord following his time in Korea. When we met up again at Fort Ord in California, I had just completed ranger school. John loves physical and mental challenges as well. He lobbied for and received a temporary assignment to Fort Benning to attend ranger school. After earning the coveted ranger tab, he returned to Fort Ord many pounds lighter—a lean, mean fighting machine. John and his wife, Kris, raised four girls. His eldest and my eldest, Tara, were born the same month in 1992. Our wives often walked together down the world-famous, picturesque 17 Mile Drive in Pebble Beach, California, with the infants in strollers.

John and I both worked at Pfizer Pharmaceuticals as sales professionals. I hired John as a sales representative when I was national sales director at Ferring Pharmaceuticals. Our friendship remained strong over the years. I looked forward to seeing John and taking a trip down memory lane. We reminisced about Army life, Pfizer, and Ferring, and we talked about our families. We treated ourselves to a meal at Popeyes before John dropped me off at the bike shop to retrieve Tank. I cherished the few hours I spent with Carlos and John. So many laughs, so many memories, unique lives we have lived. The weather was expected to be poor the next few days. But after a rest day in Austin, it was time to get back to the reality of cycling across the country.

October 23 – Austin to Bastrop (38 miles)

I sauntered to the window, pulled the curtain aside, and peeked outside of my motel room, hoping to see the sun, or at least no moisture falling from the sky. Unfortunately, it was drizzling, and severe storms threatened the day. We began the day riding as a group, but each settled on their own pace within a mile. I rode through several streets, like a maze, finding my way to the outer edges of Austin. The hustle and bustle of Austin were now in the rearview mirror. I rode on Burleson Road, which ran parallel to the Austin-Bergstrom Airport, and looked up at a United 737, the first airplane I had seen since leaving San Diego. As I looked up in amusement at the plane, I reflected on the hundreds of business trips I'd taken over the years. Shortly after, on State Highway 21, I passed Bastrop Memorial Stadium, capacity 6,471, a high school football stadium resembling a college stadium, with an enormous scoreboard, stands on four sides, and a parking lot that could hold hundreds of vehicles. In Texas, the passion people have for high school football is statewide. The rivalries have lasted for generations. I envisioned seeing thousands of fans in the stadium on a Friday night cheering on their high school football team.

I arrived at our KOA campsite in Bastrop, Texas, at about 5:00 p.m. The primitive camping area was completely underwater due to a flooded Colorado River resulting from the torrential rains in days prior. The KOA campsite owner moved us to a covered pavilion on higher ground. The raging muddy water covered the entire lower end of the campsite. Looking at the brown, dirty running water reminded me of the 1972 flood of Yellow Breeches Creek in Camp Hill, Pennsylvania. Hurricane Agnes dropped several inches of rain, causing the Susquehanna River to overflow and flood the main tributaries, including Yellow Breeches, devastating my hometown neighborhood. I vividly remember rowing with friends in a rowboat on Tall Tree Drive and Yellow Breeches Drive, two streets that were completely submerged at the bottom of a hill close to my home. We were fortunate that the water did not flood our home. Many friends who lived on Tall Tree Drive and Yellow Breeches Drive were not so lucky.

October 24 – Bastrop to Carmine (68 miles)

We were leapfrogging across the state. Each day brought us that much closer to Louisiana. The sixty-eight-mile ride to a campground in Carmine proved extremely challenging, partly due to the 3,000-foot climb but mainly due to the challenges of wearing a rain jacket, rain pants, rain shoes, helmet cover, and gloves all day in the pouring rain. I started riding about eight that morning to Bastrop State Park, about four miles northeast of the KOA campground. What was supposed to be a nice, scenic ride through the park was not so. Joel and I entered the state park at the same time. We followed the GPS route for about two miles and saw that a bridge we were supposed to cross was closed for construction.

There was no other way around. We rode back to the entrance and asked the park ranger for an alternate route, which she directed us to. I thought about asking her why she had not mentioned anything about the bridge construction when we first passed by her, but I didn't want to know the answer, because I was irritated and didn't want to make her angry, so I didn't ask. There was nothing I could do about it. So annoying! I did not need that aggravation, so Joel and I continued riding on the alternate route.

The park was not crowded. I only saw one woman out for a morning stroll. Much of the surrounding countryside was barren, but it was not like clearcutting, where trees are uniformly cut down in a defined area of the forest. The hills were short, but the grades were steep. It is a good thing the Band-Aid fix to my chainring worked. I am convinced I could not have kept forward momentum on these hills without using the granny gear.

In 2011, a wildfire devastated over 90 percent of two-thousand-acre Bastrop State Park, turning trees into toothpicks. It was comparable to the utter devastation caused by the 1993 Laguna Hills fire in Orange County, California. On that fateful day in October 1993, I was driving south on the 405 freeway from Long Beach to Newport Beach and watched the distant skies turn red. At the time I did not realize I was watching one of the twenty largest fire losses in US history.[27] Today, I could see that green undergrowth had returned in some areas of Bastrop State Park, but large swaths of land remain burnt and brown. Many trees still showed signs of fire damage. Recovery efforts continue to this day.

I'd missed the small herd of Texas longhorns on LBJ's 1,500-acre ranch, but I finally saw one longhorn shortly after exiting the park. I kept a safe distance from the massive steer. The horns protruding from both sides of its head were a thing of beauty but something to fear. Strange though it may seem, it took seventeen days and more than six hundred miles of cycling through Texas before I saw a longhorn or an oil derrick.

About ten miles outside of Carmine, I rode through the town of Round Top (population 90). Every October, between forty and fifty thousand people descend on Round Top for an annual antique auction. It is one of the world's largest. I could not imagine how this tiny town

---

27 Portlandoregon.gov/laguna_hills_fire

hosted so many people in one gathering and where they all stayed. And considering I was in a state that boasts that everything is bigger there, I laughed when I rode by a Catholic church, a ridiculously small church, with a sign in front claiming "Wellington, Texas, home to the world's smallest Catholic church."

My legs were tired. I was wet, cold, and miserable when I entered the campsite in Carmine. Doug and Klaus had taken a more direct route, avoiding Bastrop State Park, and arrived in Carmine a couple of hours before I did. They found JW's Steakhouse, about a quarter mile away from the campsite, where we all got together for dinner later that night, under shelter and away from the nasty weather. The skies opened at 4:00 p.m., the same time I arrived at the campsite. It was a challenge to keep my gear dry while setting up the tent in the rain. It took me twenty minutes to finish, about ten minutes more than usual.

Because of the rain, I methodically plucked pieces of equipment one by one from the panniers, trying to keep everything dry. Usually, when arriving at camp, I unloaded everything on the ground at once, making the setup process much easier and faster. My Big Agnes tent, made of ripstop nylon with mixed denier fabric for extra tear strength and puncture resistance, was about to be tested again. My three-season backpacking tent was designed for rain, wind, cold, and heat, precisely for nights like tonight. A small pond situated close to my tent site attracted mosquitos; they were out in force and started biting as soon as I began raising my tent.

October 25 – Carmine to Navasota (44 miles)

The rain stopped around 3:00 a.m., which made breaking down camp easier than I had expected. I slept okay but woke up to nasty mosquitos, high humidity, and a light mist. I quickly packed my dank, soggy gear. I jammed items into one pannier until it was full and then filled the other three until everything was loaded and Tank was ready to go. I knew the added weight from wet clothing would increase pedaling toil. There was no alternative; I just needed to press on. The first problem of the day: my glasses fogged incessantly. Trying to read the map, the Garmin device, or road signs was challenging. I was annoyed because to clear the fog from my glasses, I had to stop pedaling and reach into my pocket for a dry cloth to wipe the glasses clean, and within minutes I had to repeat it. This routine lasted for about half the ride to Navasota. Before leaving Carmine, I had prayed the rain would stop, the humidity would drop, and Tank would fix itself! But deep down, I embraced the arduous riding conditions. My level of fulfillment increased exponentially during and throughout the most taxing days on the saddle. I related to and agreed with the old proverb "There is no gain without pain." My journey to St. Augustine would be more rewarding the more demanding the path was to get there.

I tried to put Carmine out of my mind as soon as I left the campsite that morning. Sleeping on the ground during the storm was the most miserable experience I had the entire trip, by far. "This weather sucks, and this campsite is the worst," I firmly asserted to the group prior to leaving.

Travis interjected, "It must be bad if *you're* complaining. This is the first time I've heard you say anything negative since meeting you in San Diego."

"It was nasty weather. I have to keep it real," I responded.

It took me a few minutes to gather my thoughts and refocus on the day ahead. Thinking about reaching the 2,000-mile mark helped shape my mindset for the ride. Eighteen straight days in Texas meant that the Louisiana state border could not be too far away. I was the second, after Joel, to arrive at camp in Navasota, Texas. Others arrived sporadically, but all well before sunset. I set up camp at the RV park on the west side of town. The sun shone brightly; a gentle land breeze arose a couple of hours before sunset. The draft supplied the right amount of air to dry our wet clothing. I cleaned my riding shorts at the local laundromat, two miles from the campsite, still mindful of the saddle sores that continued to cause minor irritation.

After dinner, we all watched the sunset for the first time in several days, a pleasant change from the never-ending grey skies that dominated the previous twelve days and nights. I woke up in the middle of the night to the loud sound of a train approaching Navasota from several miles away. Eventually, the rumbling turned to the piercing whistle that travels long-distance in the wide-open desert. The siren blew for fifteen seconds, which seemed like an eternity. I could not imagine living in Navasota and trying to sleep through that whistle every night. We woke up to a beautiful sunrise. (I heard about Navasota again, several weeks after riding through town, when former President Bush died on November 30, 2018. A train carrying his body passed through Navasota on the way to his final resting place at his Presidential Library and Museum in College Station, Texas.)

At some point between Del Rio and Navasota, it hit me that I could complete the coast-to-coast ride. I realized I was a strong rider. Somewhere during those 325 miles, my focus had changed; I was no longer satisfied just to have acted on my dream. I was consumed with a desire to finish every inch of the ride on the saddle. Paradoxically, I began to worry that a mechanical issue would derail me. "What ifs" entered my mind often. What would I do if I was injured? What would I do if my saddle sores became infected?

From the time I left San Diego through the first three weeks on the road, I rarely thought about St. Augustine. A couple of challenging days early on helped sharpen my thinking to stay focused on what was ahead that day. I thought back to riding through the California desert, the Arizona heat, the New Mexico mountains, and Texas's never-ending roads. I was pleased to have made it this far, but not satisfied. I had a mission to complete. I never lost sight of the big picture. Every so often, my mind flashed to a video I'd watched before leaving of someone finishing the final leg of the Southern Tier, entering St. Augustine to no fanfare, no bells, no whistles, nothing. Just the satisfaction of knowing they completed an epic journey. In the beginning, I did not know what to expect. That was no longer the situation. I had experienced mountains, heat, desert, humidity, wind, rain, and cold. I tackled each day with vigor. I could not imagine anything forcing me onto the sidelines.

October 26 – Navasota to Cagle Recreation Area (39 miles)

The roads east of Navasota are part of the Texas Ironman training route. I prepared for a lot of climbing and focused my mind on the task ahead. The group stopped at Snowflake Donuts in downtown Navasota to fill up on sugar before the big day unfolded. I had surprised myself by not seeking out more donut shops in the rural communities I rode through. Any day that included a visit to either a barbershop, a coffee shop, an ice cream shop, or a donut shop was always a good day.

It was a beautiful start to the day: sun shining, wind at our backs, paved roads, and very few cars for miles. Cycling on State Highway 149, I genuinely appreciated the time off from work.

I thought of Emma answering the phone the first time I called the ACA to inquire about the ride. Emma put me at ease and politely informed me that at fifty-six years of age, I would be one of the group's younger members. I began thinking about how I would describe what it's like riding a bike across the country. As odd as it may sound, completing a coast-to-coast bike ride is much more achievable than many people realize. Preparation is important. Riding with the proper equipment is crucial. Having a passion for cycling helps but is not necessary. Being physically fit is essential, but not to the level I'd thought. Time is the greatest challenge. Not many people have three months to walk away from work or their family to take on such an adventure. But the physical challenge can be overcome and was easier than I initially thought possible.

I developed a cycling rhythm a few hundred miles after leaving San Diego. My body acclimated to being on the saddle for many hours at a time. My legs and knees were sore the first few days, but the morning I left Quartzsite, Arizona, on September 22, most of the soreness in my legs, stiffness in my knees, and pain had disappeared. Except for one morning in Louisiana and a couple of days close to the finish in St. Augustine, my body held up extremely well.

After crossing into New Mexico, there were days when I completed rides of fifty to sixty miles, and it just did not seem too difficult anymore. There were days I arrived at camp and wished I could continue because I still had plenty of gas in my tank. It was as if I was riding myself into shape, a concept several experienced cyclists described in various articles I read when preparing for the journey. Oddly enough, cycling oneself into shape is a valid notion.

I averaged fifty-five miles (ranging from forty to eighty) and six to seven hours on the saddle each day. My average speed while cycling was approximately ten miles per hour, which is achievable for many inexperienced long-distance cyclists. Mechanical issues, unforeseen injuries, and extreme weather events all raise the stakes for a successful journey. In general, the mental stamina requirements are more challenging than the physical demands. The daily grind took a toll on my psyche at times. The most significant concern I had was numbness in my hands (and feet), known as handlebar palsy. Even though I often moved my hands into various positions, the constant and prolonged pressure on the ulnar sensory nerve caused significant discomfort.[28] I remained disciplined from the beginning (minus a few lapses), executing my strategy, breaking the entire ride down into ten-mile segments. I conquered a series of short victories each day. That I did not allow my mind to wander and think about St. Augustine required tremendous discipline.

Before arriving at the Cagle Recreation Area campsite, I rode over a bridge spanning Lake Conroe and stopped to take in the picturesque backdrop of sunshine and lush green trees surrounding crystal-clear water. Located forty-five miles north of Houston, the campground is a destination for city dwellers escaping the hustle and bustle of city life

---

28 www.handsurgeonsnyc/cyclists-palsy-handlebar-palsy

on the weekends. I expected the campground to be more crowded than it was on this Friday night.

Travis, who had separated from the group after leaving Bastrop a few days earlier, rejoined us after fixing his derailleur, which broke while climbing a hill outside of Bastrop. He was about to enter the state park when his derailleur broke again. This was the third time it had broken on the trip. A Good Samaritan transported him in the back of a truck to Houston, the closest place that could service his bike. He finally figured out that the BOB trailer was not compatible with the rear derailleur assembly, resulting in constant mechanical problems. Travis had more mechanical issues than anyone else but always kept a positive spirit. We were all pleased to see him when he arrived at the campsite.

Because critters roam at night, I placed the food for breakfast and lunch inside the bathroom building to secure it overnight. Milk, cold cuts, yogurt, and fruit were all stored in a cold (insulated) bag. I woke up well before sunrise and went to retrieve the food. Something did not look right when, in my grogginess, I entered the bathroom and turned on the light. I could not pinpoint what it was. It finally dawned on me that the cold bag was missing. I walked back to the picnic table where we'd eaten dinner the night before, thinking someone must have already retrieved the cold bag. It was not there. Finally, after scouring the surrounding campsite for fifteen minutes, I stopped looking for it. It was gone, nowhere to be found. We did not go hungry, though. We had plenty of food that did not require refrigeration. We guessed who was responsible. Was it a four-legged critter? More likely, the culprit had two legs. There was not any other reasonable explanation. We were surrounded by RVs, some of which cost hundreds of thousands of dollars. The missing food was not the issue. Who would want a stinking cold bag?!

We did not dwell on the missing bag. After eating and cleaning, it was time to distribute the group gear. Standing next to the picnic table, reaching down to pick up an item, Wally shouted, "Hey, who carries the bag of bags?" (the name of one of the items). I looked up at Wally and started laughing. It dawned on me we had invented names for the group gear that only we riders would understand. I did not realize (until Wally yelled) how comical it was to name each item. It was one of those times when I just shook my head and laughed at the situation. (I carried the bag of utensils, Tom the cold bag, Joel the pots and pans; I do not remember who carried the bag of stuff or the bag of bags.)

October 27 – Cagle Recreation Area to Shepherd (46 miles)

For the next thirty-seven miles, I rode through the Bible Belt on Highway 150. Between the Cagle campground and Coldspring, Texas, I saw more churches than in any other stretch of road the entire trip. The churches were all tiny. The parking lots were small enough to hold no more than twenty cars. Unlike the hundreds of people that filled the pews at St. Theresa's Catholic Church in New Cumberland, Pennsylvania, where I attended growing up, I am sure the churches I rode by were only large enough for fifty congregants to sit comfortably. The few churches I entered had a single aisle with pews on both sides and no more than ten rows.

Coldspring was full of activity when I arrived, with people walking in and out of stores and on the sidewalk. Music bellowed from large tents set up next to the municipal building in the center of town. The most massive Texas state flag I had ever seen was flying in the breeze.

About fifteen miles further east of Coldspring, I entered the town of Shepherd. I glanced to my left and saw something I had not seen in 1,928 miles: two people playing basketball under a pavilion. I stopped, walked closer to them, and placed my bike on the grass. I introduced myself to a man who was about sixty years old. I started by saying, "This will be a bizarre introduction, but I want to share my story of how I got to the town of Shepherd." He walked toward me, away from the young teenage girl he was shooting with, stood in front of me, and glared. He did not say anything. He seemed to be shielding me from speaking to the girl.

I proceeded to tell him, "I injured my foot playing basketball a few months ago. I tried to run on it after a few weeks of rehab. My foot did not heal well, so for exercise, I decided to ride my bike. Then I decided to ride my bike across the country, and now I'm here…"

He continued listening intently to what I had to say but did not say or do anything. It was the first time I was unsuccessful in breaking the ice and carrying on a conversation with someone on this trip. It was an awkward moment, at least for me. I kept talking. I told him I was from New Jersey. At this point, he raised his eyebrows. He chimed in, "I'm originally from New Jersey, a retired police officer from Patterson." That explained his reservation! He told me that he moved to Texas after retirement to be closer to his children and grandchildren. From that point on, we had a pleasant conversation. He told me his granddaughter was practicing, preparing for basketball season. I asked if I could get a picture with him and his granddaughter, emphasizing the poignancy of the moment. His granddaughter did not want to be photographed but did agree to take a picture of me with her grandfather. After the photo, we shook hands and said goodbye, and he wished me well as I walked back to Tank.

I looked to my left and saw Earl Brown, mayor of Shepherd, standing there campaigning for San Jacinto County Judge. The election was a couple of weeks away. Signs dotted the landscape. He stood next to his campaign sign: "Democrats and Republicans United … Vote for Earl Brown. People Over Party." It had a nice ring to it. Earl seemed like a great guy. A few of the locals I spoke to later that day told me they saw Earl every morning at the local coffee shop. The phrase "All politics is local," strongly associated with the late Speaker of the United States House of Representatives, came to mind. I had also been keeping track of the national political scene by signage. Ted Cruz's signs dominated rural communities. Beto O'Rourke signs were predominant in Austin.

I had ten more miles to go before arriving at my destination, the Shepherd Sanctuary. The only word that accurately describes the Shepherd Sanctuary is *funky*. Statues of the Venus de Milo, the Virgin

Mary, and Sasquatch are placed in the flower beds, adding to the eclectic (some might say jumbled) grounds. We had a choice between sleeping in cabins or pitching tents in the communal area next to a fire pit. An outdoor shower and exposed bathroom added to the granola feel. The manager told me the sanctuary's vision was to create an experience aligned with a progressive approach to life instead of the traditional way that dominated the surrounding area. When I shared with the manager the story about meeting the retired police officer at the pavilion, she put everything into perspective for me. Months before, in a town about forty miles north of Shepherd, a young girl was kidnapped in a Walmart parking lot. I immediately realized why the guy had been so standoffish when I approached him and his granddaughter.

My short stay at the sanctuary was enjoyable. Touring with the ACA is a terrific way to go. I would never have found the Shepherd Sanctuary on my own.

The Southern Tier route is an often-traveled cross-country route. People are accustomed to seeing cyclists riding through their town. I was still amused at the reaction of so many. When I met a gas station attendant or convenience store employee and told them about the ride, expressions were priceless. Some just looked and said, "Say what?" Others said, "That's a long way." Others simply furrowed their brows with that puzzled look. I loved seeing the reactions.

October 28 – Shepherd to Silsbee (60 miles)

A fantastic day on the saddle was followed by a fun night staying at the Shepherd Sanctuary. The camber of the smoothly paved roads, with broad shoulders, favorable tailwinds, and light traffic on Highway 787 led me to believe I could break my full-day speed record, 18.75 miles per hour (on the fifty-five miles between Marathon, Texas, and Sanderson, Texas). I gave it my best but fell short by 2.75 miles per hour, averaging 16 miles per hour for sixty miles. When conditions were right, like they were on this day, it felt like I was gliding. Crossing the 2,000-mile marker put me in an entirely different mindset. I was out of the mountains and cruising along the coastal plains. I thought, "The homestretch, only 1,000 miles to go."

On my ride this day approaching the Louisiana border, I took a trip down memory lane. We had begun riding at sea level in San Diego forty days before, climbed 2,000 feet riding the rugged mountains east of San Diego, then descended below sea level for a couple of days, eventually climbing to 8,000 feet before settling in at 3,500 feet before the gradual descent upon arriving in eastern Texas.

Transitioning from eastern Texas to western Louisiana would bring a new set of challenges, primarily dealing with aggressive dogs that run loose and are not shy about attacking cyclists. During the map meeting the night before we left the Sanctuary, Joyce told the group to prepare for a dog encounter shortly after leaving in the morning. A dog that lived at a house about half a mile away from the Sanctuary had been known to attack other ACA tour groups. Dog encounters happen fast. I prepared for the rendezvous by holding a new foghorn (which I bought at a Walmart in Del Rio) in my right hand. I rode point when we left the Sanctuary at about 7:30 a.m. Others were not far behind. I turned on my GoPro to capture all the excitement that was about to unfold. While I quietly rode on a side street toward the intersection where we expected to confront the aggressive dog, several other dogs sat quietly outside of their homes staring at us. Perhaps they were spotters for the aggressive dog up ahead? I approached the intersection, picked up my pace, held the horn in my right hand, and turned left on the main street in front of the suspected house. The morning was quiet, eerily quiet. When I made it safely by the house, I was relieved but at the same time felt slighted for all the anticipation, planning, and discussion about what to do if the dog came at your ankle, tire, pannier, etc. My adrenaline was pumping. We had all needlessly psyched ourselves up for the non-encounter.

I continued to meet many interesting people. At the AM Donut Shop off Highway 59 in Cleveland, Texas, I met a guy named Buzzy. He told me he'd cycled one hundred miles a couple of days earlier. He pointed to his motorcycle and quipped, "My bike has a motor." Shortly after, at the same donut shop, two women cyclists, Mackenzie and Joanna, walked in and offered to pay for my coffee. They had noticed my bike leaning up against a support beam outside the shop and began telling me about their cycling experience. I stopped a customer before he walked out and asked him to take a picture of me with Mackenzie, Joanna, and their small Chihuahua. Coffee in hand, the three of us walked outside. Joanna pointed to her Surly Tour bike and proudly shared with me that she'd ridden fifty miles the previous weekend. They were intrigued by my cross-country ride, and Joanna asked, "How long do you ride each day? Have you had any flat tires?" I gave her the lowdown on my trip thus far. "I'd love to ride across the country as well. Maybe someday," she said.

Tank, fully loaded and ready to go, and Joanna's Surly, sporting a handlebar bag, lock, and old-fashioned handlebar bike bell, provided a perfect backdrop for a final photo before saying goodbye and riding our separate ways. I could not make out the brand of Mackenzie's bike, but I saw an empty cage in front of the handlebars. I chalked the meeting up to another unplanned encounter that kept me searching for the next. Joanna and Mackenzie rode off with their pooch in Mackenzie's front handlebar basket.

Often, random encounters triggered a thought or memory. I would latch onto a train of thought and stay with it for as long as I could. These ladies and their dog reminded me of Dorothy and Toto in *The Wizard of Oz*. My thoughts went from Toto to the Lion, the Scarecrow, the Tin Man, and one of the main lessons from *The Wizard of Oz*: we all have the qualities we need to be successful, and the search for enlightenment does not need to involve a trip down the Yellow Brick Road. Was the Southern Tier my Yellow Brick Road? Was the nasty weather in Texas the Wicked Witch? Were the energizing encounters with hundreds of real people my Good Witch?

I thought of my kids; I could not wait to share my stories with them. If their dad could ride a bike across the country when others thought he was a little crazy, they could do whatever they wanted in life and not concern themselves with how others viewed their decisions.

The group arrived at the Red Cloud RV Park outside of Silsbee with plenty of sunlight remaining to set up camp. Three of us watched the NFL on TV for about fifteen minutes before settling in for an early night. Doug, Travis, and Klaus walked to a karaoke bar close to the campsite. Before leaving in the morning, Travis played a short video of Klaus singing the night before. Not only was Klaus a good cook, but he was also a pretty talented singer. Doug, Klaus, and Travis knew how to have an enjoyable time. I was in awe of their ability to indulge at night and ride all day.

Doug, Klaus, and Travis consumed a fifteen-pack, typically Coors, on many nights. They woke up with the rest of us and had the energy, drive, and determination to move out in the morning. My body cannot handle beer like it used to. In college and the Army, I was the one to set the pace. Not anymore. Cycling fifty-five miles per day on average was tough enough. I could not imagine waking up every day with a headache and riding with less than one hundred percent of my energy. I declined each time they offered me a beer. My excuse: I was waiting until the celebration dinner the night before arriving in St. Augustine to enjoy a cold one.

A good night's sleep was a precursor to good riddance to the state of Texas in the morning. But when we woke, Tom saw that his back tire was flat. It took us about fifteen minutes to figure out the cause was a slow leak. A tiny piece of steel had punctured the tire—the result of riding over shredded truck tire debris the day before. Tom replaced the inner tube, and then we all left the Red Cloud RV Park.

Chapter 5

LOUISIANA (GUMBO, HURRICANES, AND CAN YOU BELIEVE IT?)

October 29 – Silsbee to Merryville (53 miles)

We had been on the road for six weeks, three in Texas alone. There was heavy traffic early in the morning when we left Silsbee. Broad shoulders made cycling a little less stressful, but my attention was on dodging glass, metal, and shredded tires strewn over the road. About ten miles into our ride, I looked up and saw Joel about 150 yards in front of me, and two dogs were running toward him from the right. It was hard to tell how close the dogs got to Joel. It did not look like they made contact. I knew they would chase me next. The dogs stopped, turned around, and looked at me. I picked up my pace and held my new dog horn in my right hand. The dogs ran toward me, and when they were about thirty yards away, they started running directly at me. I raised my right hand, reached out with the horn pointing in their direction, and gave it a push. The sound of the foghorn stopped them dead in their tracks. We growled at each other as I passed. Not this time, I thought to myself.

I became overly excited when I saw a road sign signaling that DeRidder, Louisiana, was twenty-six miles east of my current location. "How cool is that!" I thought. The countless times I rode through DeRidder on my way to Lake Charles for weekend parties when I was stationed at Fort Polk, Louisiana, flashed through my mind. A little further east, I crossed Quicksand Creek, the Louisiana state border, and entered Beauregard Parish. I stopped, turned around, and looked west at a stone structure in the shape of the state of Texas. It was a state welcoming sign for people traveling in the opposite direction. It was a striking contrast to when, three weeks before, I had unknowingly crossed the Texas border.

On Highway 190, I rode by dilapidated trailer homes, condemned vacant buildings, and many logging trucks passing in both directions. Wood shavings from passing trucks flew off due to the wind, often dropping to the ground close to me. The woody scent of sawdust and barking dogs were more hints I had crossed into the state of Louisiana.

One of the most enjoyable places I visited was the Merryville Historical Society & Museum in Merryville, Louisiana. On the property is the original Burks family log cabin, built in 1883. It is on the National Register of Historic Places and is the only authentic log cabin in Beauregard Parish.[29] The museum building, located next to the cabin, houses local history and has many military exhibits scattered throughout.[30] Eddy and Renee, volunteers who run the museum and our hosts for the evening, served us a feast like no other. We had chicken and sausage gumbo—eight gallons of it, with all the fixings. When Eddy announced, "Yawl suppa's ready," I knew we were in for a treat.

During supper, Eddy and Renee shared information about the surrounding area. Major General Patton, in command of the 2nd Armored Division, took part in the Louisiana Maneuvers of 1941, written up as one of the greatest military events in history. The maneuvers

---

29 National Register of Historic Places: Burks House, National Park Service, 2018

30 Merryvillehistoricalmusuem.org

helped to prepare the United States Army for World War II. When General Patton left Louisiana after many of his units moved through local Louisiana communities, including Merryville, he left stories with the local folks that have been told over the years.[31]

And my mind was blown when Eddy told us that Mardi Gras in New Orleans is not an authentic celebration. The real deal takes place in the Deep South, in towns such as Mamou, Louisiana.

The real Mardi Gras begins at 4:00 a.m. when beer trucks follow along as people go from place to place securing ingredients for the gumbo that is served at the end of the day. By the time late afternoon rolls around, one can only imagine how people act after a full day within arm's length of a beer truck. (The Southern Tier route passes through Mamou, but unfortunately not during Mardi Gras.)

Alligators and snakes (coral, copperhead, water moccasin, chicken, and cottonmouth) inhabit the area. Panthers are present, too. Merryville used to be a thriving community, but as with many small towns along the route, times are tough as they transition to a new tourism economy. Paper mills and logging remain vital today, evidenced by the many trucks that passed me on Highway 190 heading east toward St. Augustine.

I met Renee and Eddy's eighth-grade son, a football player. I showed him a picture of Brian. I tried not to think about home. I missed my family terribly, but my desire to finish had not faded at all.

While I enjoyed learning about Merryville's history, my favorite part of our conversation centered around college football and the big LSU-versus-Nebraska game scheduled for the upcoming weekend. Renee was an LSU fan. Eddy's team was Nebraska. We all loved listening to their discussion about the upcoming game. I kept quiet about my Penn State football allegiance. I knew it would not have gone over too well, especially since Penn State was robbed of a share of the title in 1994 when Nebraska "won" the National Championship.

---

31 Leesvilledailyleader.com

Folks in Merryville considered the area north of Highway 190 to be Yankee country. Merryville is literally on the southern tip (six tenths of a mile) of Highway 190. It would be no different than living half a mile south of the Mason–Dixon Line and thinking of neighbors to the north as foreigners. I was not about to divulge my football preference or my Pennsylvania roots.

It was such an enjoyable visit I did not want it to end. Renee and Eddy served a breakfast of pancakes, eggs, bacon, juice, coffee, and all the fixings. It was time to go, but not before one more fiasco. Before leaving in the morning, I forgot to close the door to the outdoor bathroom. Eddy, Renee, and others in my cycling group laughed at me as I did my business (number one) in plain sight for everyone to see.

October 30 – Merryville to Oberlin (58 miles)

I made it to DeRidder, Louisiana, at 11:00 a.m. Crossing the Louisiana state border brought me back to 1984. After receiving my Army commission as a 2nd lieutenant upon college graduation, I moved to Louisiana (after a short stint at Fort Rucker, Alabama, and Fort Bliss, Texas). I began my first active-duty assignment at Fort Polk outside Leesville, Louisiana. I used to drive my car through DeRidder on my way to Lake Charles for weekend parties. Some memories had faded. Others were clear, like the day I signed in to my unit at the 5th Division Headquarters building at Fort Polk, Louisiana. As I crossed the street from the parking lot headed toward the HQ entrance, I passed in front of the commanding general's vehicle, with the general inside. I was about to learn an important lesson.

As I waited to in-process (military jargon for starting a new job), a captain walked up and asked me to follow him. I remember him saying, "You're about to meet the commanding general of the 5th Division, Major General Leuer." I did not know what was going on. I knocked on the door. The general invited me into his office. I stood at attention and saluted (that much I knew). He asked several questions, including how long I had been on the post. After hearing I'd arrived earlier that same day, he told me why I was in his office. The protocol is to salute the general's vehicle when it is occupied and the American flag is attached to the front of it. I had not done that. He counseled me about setting a good example; I would soon lead a platoon of thirty-nine soldiers. He wished me well and dismissed me. I never made that mistake again.

The meeting with Major General Leuer was the beginning of my adult working life. Shortly after taking over the platoon, I met Greg, a recent graduate from the Military Academy at West Point. We quickly became friends and roommates. Another friend named Jeter, a graduate of West Point assigned to the 34th Combat Engineer Battalion, the same as Greg, also became a close friend. Jeter and I competed in mini-triathlons and bonded over many late nights and early mornings. The vast majority of newly commissioned second lieutenants bought new cars with their newfound guaranteed monthly income. Greg and I spent many weekends changing oil and washing our cars (mine a practical Honda Accord LX and Greg's a sporty Datsun 280zx), maintaining the one piece of property we owned that was not government-issued.

One of my favorite memories was when we defeated Greg and Jeter's unit in the post-basketball championship game. It was a close game. Their big man and company commander went up for an easy bucket on the left low post. I timed my jump perfectly and blocked it off the backboard to help seal the win. Our team, C Battery-155 ADA, celebrated, having just completed an unlikely run to the post title. A picture of that team is proudly displayed in my home office today.

My secret to proving credibility with the thirty-nine soldiers I led as a twenty-two-year-old newly commissioned 2nd lieutenant (affectionately called "butter bars" because the rank insignia looks like a bar of butter and because 2nd lieutenants have about the same value as a stick of butter) was to connect with them on the athletic field. The vast majority of soldiers I led were young African American men, many of whom were still pursuing a general education degree (GED). Many found solace on the basketball court or football field. Military service and athletic competition are two disciplines that bring out the best in people. When combined, the bonds formed by individuals are bone-deep—all brothers in arms. That kind of respect and trust are hard to replicate in the civilian world.

We played tackle football without pads. I wanted the ball so the soldiers could try to pummel me to the ground. I gained their respect by running through them and then reaching down to help them off the ground. I gained their respect by playing a basketball game after splitting my lip open, teeth exposed, in the posts' semifinals championship game. I put a butterfly bandage on and continued playing (I look back now and realize that was not the best decision). After the semifinal game, I received several stitches and then played the finals with a significant bandage covering half of my face. I also volunteered to carry the Oozlefinch (the Air Defense Artillery mascot) on the weekly battalion training runs. It was made of wood, weighed several pounds, and was awkward to carry.

The parallels to my bike ride were eerily familiar. I was undoubtedly the "butter bar" on this journey. I did not try to pretend I knew much about long-distance cycling. I helped the group by highlighting my physical strength and positive attitude. Carrying the heavy group gear bag and keeping a can-do approach through all the ups and downs propelled me to DeRidder, Louisiana. I had begun to question why it took a bike ride across the country to bring clarity to aspects of my recent life. But I was happy to be in the present. That much I knew.

As much fun as I had when stationed at Fort Polk, I wanted a change after two years. What became a pattern, I volunteered to go to Korea for a hardship tour. I connected with Mr. Fish (Air Defense Artillery placement officer at the Pentagon) and requested a new assignment. Soon I was on a plane to Seoul, Korea. All of this flashed through my mind in DeRidder.

A mosquito had bitten my lower leg days earlier at the Carmine KOA. It hurt when I touched the quarter-sized swollen red area, the redness expanding each day. I thought it was infected, and I was concerned it would get worse, so I stopped at the DeRidder walk-in clinic. I was the only one there at the time, so they allowed me to bring Tank inside for safekeeping. It took less than five minutes for the nurse practitioner to diagnose the problem and order a different prescription than the one I was given in Austin. She told me the cause could have been the mosquito bite or any number of other things. Either way, it was important to keep it clean and take the antibiotic as prescribed. (I was prescribed cephalexin in Austin, a cephalosporin antibiotic, and doxycycline in DeRidder, a tetracycline-class antibiotic). I now had in my possession two antibiotics in case the infection worsened.

About forty miles east of DeRidder, I saw a sign for Oakdale, Louisiana. My mind jumped to 1985, again when I was stationed at Fort Polk. One late afternoon during a field training exercise, my driver made a wrong turn in our World War II style Jeep, affectionately known as a "1/4-ton," while searching for the TOC (tactical operations center). We entered the town of Oakdale. My driver, a nineteen-year-old African American man from Louisiana, turned to me and said, "Sir, we need to get out of here." It did not take me long to realize why. He turned the Jeep, regained our bearings, and eventually made it to the TOC. I remember asking myself why people treat others so poorly because of skin color. That is not how my folks raised me.

One of my favorite pictures, displayed in my office today, is of this young soldier's arm wrapped around my shoulder after we won the post-championship basketball game. A brother in arms, literally. It made me sick to think that this young private first class was concerned about driving through Oakdale. What is wrong with some people?

October 31 – Oberlin to Chicot State Park (54 miles)

Every morning as I saddled up and set out for a new destination, I reflected on the journey that came before. The places I saw. The people I met. The clarity, the details, the roads, people's names, all of it is still crystal-clear years later. Events, situations, and people pop into my mind as I relive my journey authoring this book.

I also wondered whom I would meet, what I would see as I continued my trek across the country.

I rode into the heart of Cajun Country, finally off Highway 190 and onto Highway 128, heading east toward Mamou, Louisiana. I saw crawfish-harvesting fields on both sides of the highway. Small harvests of crawfish occur in southern states in warm waters during the warm-weather season. Louisiana is by far the largest producer of crawfish in the United States. The crawfish harvesting season runs from January through early July, and it peaks in March, April, and May, so I did not see much. Catholic churches were predominant, typically next to an above-ground cemetery. Highway 190 roads had been smooth and nicely paved. However, after crossing from Allen Parish into Evangeline Parish along Highway 128, I was once again met with bumpy, poorly maintained roads like Evan Hewes Highway in California. I also thought about the movie *Southern Comfort*, which I watched before driving to Fort Polk, Louisiana, in 1984 to begin my assignment with the 5th Mechanized Infantry Division. The 1981 film featuring the Louisiana National Guard on weekend maneuvers in Cajun Country left me with the impression that the state is all swampland. The movie portrayal did not share the full picture of the Louisiana I came to know. A lot of marshland, yes. But I met many great people, and, as a young Army soldier, I took advantage of everything Louisiana had to offer.

As I thought back to my two years living in Leesville, Louisiana, a sense of gratitude entered my mind. What a life I had lived up until this point. I had paved my own path and along the journey exposed myself to an America that is amazing in so many ways. My adult journey began in 1984, crisscrossing the country (and the world), eventually landing me in Capitola, California, on Memorial Day weekend in 1990, where I met Kelley. Now, here I was again, back to the future, having flashbacks and enjoying every minute.

As I approached the town of Mamou, I saw several signs on a lawn facing the street supporting a particular candidate running for office in the upcoming election. It dawned on me that everyone running for something had the same last name: Fontenot.

As I continued riding, I saw a group of people underneath a pavilion on the left side of the road. It looked like the group was engrossed in a morning conversation. I waved. One person waved back. I turned around and decided to visit them for a few minutes. The pavilion was attached to a community home. A few individuals asked me questions about the bike ride. One of them shared a story about learning to ride a bike with training wheels. Another person pointed at my bike and asked, "Where is the motor?" The experience of meeting these intellectually disabled individuals certainly allowed me to reflect on things and appreciate what life has to offer. I took a selfie group picture and continued to my next destination in downtown Mamou, the Krazy Cajun Café, for a big bowl of gumbo.

The Krazy Cajun Café is a well-known rest stop in the long-distance cycling community. On this day, downtown Mamou was noticeably quiet. Except for the café, the town did not appear to have much more to offer. It seemed strange that many businesses were closed late Wednesday morning. Before entering the small town, I sent a picture of one of the guys running for office to a friend of mine with the same last name, Fontenot. I remembered my friend telling me he grew up in a small town in Louisiana. When I sent the picture, I informed him I was riding through Mamou on my bike ride across the country. He texted back telling me that his Grandma lived in Mamou. "What a small world," I thought. And it was about to get much smaller.

I leaned my bike against the window in front of the Krazy Cajun Café. I walked inside and met the waitress. "Hi, I'm Larry. Is this the famous Krazy Cajun Café I've heard so much about? Did anyone else from my group stop in today?"

As we shook hands, she responded, "I'm Sylvia. No, you're the first one today." I sat down and ordered a cup of coffee and a bowl of gumbo. While the gumbo was being prepared, Sylvia brought my coffee, and before she walked away, I asked, "What's with the name Fontenot? Seems like everyone running for office has the same last name."

She responded, "Fontenot is my maiden name."

I pulled out my phone and called my friend. He picked up and, after a brief "Hi, how are you doing?" I dove right in. "I'm in Mamou. I'm going to give the phone to Sylvia, my waitress at the Krazy Cajun Café. Her maiden name is Fontenot. Maybe you guys are related." I handed the phone to Sylvia and listened to my friend and Sylvia exchange words, both trying to figure out if there was a local family connection. Their conversation shifted to a specific event that occurred in Mamou. I then looked on in disbelief (as did two coworkers of Sylvia's) as I heard Sylvia and my friend discuss details of a murder that occurred in Mamou in the mid-1980s. It turned out Sylvia's brother-in-law murdered my friend's godfather. Sylvia's husband testified against his brother at the trial. Sylvia handed me the phone after they completed their conversation. My friend asked me, "Did you get all that?" I was speechless. After a brief chat, we hung up, and I chalked this story up as another unforgettable moment on my journey across the country.

Before leaving the Krazy Cajun Café, I saw a disturbed homeless woman walking alone outside. Sylvia mentioned that the lady used to be a respected nurse practitioner in town. Tough times had taken a toll on her. It was sad to see.

On this night, we stayed at a small cabin about five miles off-route in the Chicot State Park. For the last mile before arriving at the cabin, I rode on a narrow gravel and dirt path surrounded by forest. The forest reminded me of the film *The Blair Witch Project*, except, luckily, we had bikes on which to escape. Fierce winds, hail, and a potential tornado were forecast throughout the night. The tornado was not my concern, though. I wondered how the ride leaving the cabin in the morning on a muddy dirt road would be if the storm were as bad as predicted.

We celebrated Halloween night by roasting a ham in the cabin's oven, consuming plenty of candy, and choosing not to watch *The Blair Witch Project*. Riding on the dirt road the following morning was not as difficult as I expected. A lot of rain had fallen, but I managed to dodge the water-filled potholes and leave the park with a relatively clean bike.

It was surprising to me that no one in our group had been injured after riding two thousand miles. On busy highways and country roads with limited visibility, everyone had safely navigated through hundreds, if not thousands, of opportunities where a vehicle could have accidentally clipped one of us, but we had all stayed safe.

November 1 – Chicot State Park to Simmesport (47 miles)

I trailed the group the day we left Chicot State Park. About five miles into the ride, I saw Doug, Travis, and Klaus stopped in front of me. Travis had clipped Klaus's bike from behind. Travis tumbled to the ground but luckily was not hurt, although the rear derailleur was damaged again (for the fourth time). Doug, a mechanical engineer by training and bike whisperer by choice, fixed the derailleur in no time. Doug builds bikes at his home in Minnesota. He's a good guy to have along on a self-contained cross-country touring group.

I confronted a lot of aggressive dogs in the western part of Louisiana. After a few encounters, I finally settled on a defensive strategy that seemed to work for me. As soon as I saw a dog running toward me, I readied my foghorn and, at the right moment, when the dog(s) were about twenty feet away, I blew the horn, which startled them, giving me enough time to accelerate. The dogs usually retreated after I rode past their property line. They're just doing their job, protecting their owner's property, and do not realize the road in front is public. There are not visible fences creating a boundary that keeps dogs from leaving the property line. Often, several large dogs chased me, and most of them looked healthy. The discordance between living in poverty and having the expense of caring for multiple large dogs occupied my mind riding through much of Louisiana.

Trash littered the sides of many Louisiana roads—the garbage piled up in gullies or canals that ran parallel to houses. On occasion, a beautifully well-kept house popped up, but despair categorized the surrounding community more than any other word. Every so often, a "do not litter" sign appeared with the threat of a fine for noncompliance. These communities did not enforce their laws. I could not imagine waking up every day, looking outside my home, and seeing a bunch of trash scattered in the canals across the street from my property. It was disappointing to see such a lack of concern. Although so much is out of our control, a simple thing like picking up trash seems so basic and doable. Where was the pride?

We slept on the floor of a kitchen inside a Catholic church in Simmesport, Louisiana. Instead of cooking dinner, the group voted to eat at Rabalais Seafood Restaurant. I walked by houses that displayed the Confederate flag in the front yard on my one-mile walk to the restaurant. Living in the Northeast for as long as I had, it took a while to get used to seeing Confederate flags flying full staff.

Soon I would be back to riding on nicely paved roads east of Simmesport, Louisiana. Moreover, if everything turned out all right and the stars aligned, I hoped to get a glimpse of the rougarou, a werewolf-like creature existing in Cajun folklore and found in the swamps and bayous of Louisiana.[32] "Only in Louisiana," I thought. Before returning to the church after dinner, Joel, Travis, Doug, Klaus, and I set foot inside the Y-Not Stop family-owned store next to the restaurant, searching for ice cream. "We sure do," one of the employees replied when Travis asked if they sold ice cream. While a woman prepared each of our orders, a young man talked to the rest of us about our trip across the country. He told us where the best locations were to see local wildlife, specifically alligators and the rougarou east of Simmesport, on our way to the Mississippi.

"What's the deal with the rougarou?" I asked, as if seeing a rougarou was no different than seeing a buffalo run wild in Yellowstone Park.

The employee continued, "Legend has it, pay attention when you ride by the Morganza Spillway (a flood-control structure built after the Mississippi Flood of 1927, the most destructive in United States

---

32 Nolaweekend.com_beware_of_Rougarou

history[33]). That's the best place to spot the Rougarou." The employee did not give details on what he meant by spotting the rougarou. I did not push the issue. The legend of the rougarou, which is known to roam in this area of Louisiana for generations, piqued my interest and kept me on my toes as I rode to the Mighty Mississippi. I focused intently, scanning the water, hoping to see the rougarou or a gator's beady eyes and head skimming the surface. But I did not see any unusual activity when I rode by the shores of many tributaries surrounding the Mississippi River.

November 2 – Simmesport to Jackson (73 miles)

A few miles before reaching the Mighty Mississippi, Tom and I stopped for lunch at a restaurant in New Roads, Louisiana, where the tasty Cajun fried chicken was outdone only by the five-star customer service. Our waitress, Patricia, was a hoot. Before I ordered food at the counter, she looked at me and then to her left and pointed to the Cajun Ten Commandments displayed on the wall next to the register. A few of my favorites: "Don't be cussin' at nobody," "Listen to yo mama an' yo daddy," "Don't be killin' no people… duck an' fish, das okay," and "Don't take nuttin' from nobody else." My absolute favorite was "Notice: This place is politically incorrect. We say Merry Christmas and one nation under God. We salute our flag and give thanks to our troops. If this offends you… leave." Nuf said—this was my type of place!

I crossed the Mississippi River over the John James Audubon Bridge. Tom and I soaked up the views at the apex before descending to the opposite side. When I started riding in San Diego, it was hard to comprehend reaching this landmark. The thought of it seemed so daunting. Now, the Mississippi River was in my rearview mirror. It was a cool feeling thinking about and processing the notion that Tank propelled me from the Pacific Ocean to the Mississippi River.

---

33 Ambrose, Stephen. "Man vs. Nature: The Great Mississippi Flood of 1927." "National Geographic." Published May 1, 2001

After crossing the Mississippi, I set my sights on Perry's Bike Hostel in Jackson, Louisiana. Joyce instructed us to be on the lookout for a small sign at the entrance to a gravel driveway off State Route 68, and "If you reach the sports bar, you've missed the hostel entrance and gone too far." I found it without any problem. The gravel road led to a small section of Perry's property that she and her husband, Lep, had turned into an outdoor tent camping area with a shower and bathroom, a way station for cyclists. There was a fire pit and a couple of picnic tables next to the sleeping area. They'd named the spot Bicycle Blvd. Each year Perry and Lep host many cross-country cyclists, groups, and individual riders. Perry is an engineer by training, a bike whisperer by choice. After dinner, sitting around the campfire with the others, she rattled off many interesting tidbits of cycling trivia. I could not keep up. She seemed willing to provide sage advice, so I asked her, "I'm trying to figure out a good trail for my wife and me to ride together. A few hundred miles, maybe a week or so on the road."

"The Natchez Trace is a good one. Highly recommend it," she offered without hesitation. Joyce had also recommended the Natchez Trace to me when I'd asked her opinion earlier in our trip.

It was a long day on the road. The group preplanned a trip to New Orleans in the morning—a sanctioned extra rest day, courtesy of the planning department of the ACA. The long-anticipated visit to New Orleans had all of us feeling good. I crawled into my tent and retired map section number five, depositing it in the bottom of my right rear pannier along with map sections one through four. "Five down, and only two more to go before reaching the Atlantic Ocean," I mused.

November 3 and 4 – New Orleans (Rest Days)

It was a big football weekend in the Bayou, LSU hosting Alabama in Baton Rouge.

The night before, while many of us sat in a circle on lawn chairs, enjoying the crackle and the intoxicating smell of burning wood around the campfire, Wally and Joyce retrieved a white, fifteen-passenger van they'd rented for the drive to New Orleans. On Saturday morning, November 3, eight well-rested, contented cyclists secured our bikes at Perry's Hostel and hopped into the van for the two-hour, 114-mile drive to New Orleans. Wally drove and Joyce was copilot. It reminded me of many trips to New Bedford, Massachusetts, in the back of the Walsh family Chevrolet station wagon in the 1960s and 1970s, adults in the front and children in the back. The difference: six adults were behaving, quiet, thinking, staring out the van windows. I thought about the Atlantic Ocean, imagined myself entering St. Augustine and dipping my tire into the surf.

We stopped at a bike mechanic's house in a neighborhood in Mid City South, Baton Rouge. Travis's derailleur continued to cause problems that needed to be addressed. The mechanic worked out of his garage. He sold any item one might need on a long bike tour. The mechanic's home (and workshop) was in the middle of a development off the beaten path. He catered to cyclists, which, it turned out, were a sizeable and very close-knit, chummy community, and this mechanic was well-known to members of the ACA, including Joyce and Wally.

The van parked in front of the Nola Jazz House on Canal Street, our lodging for one night in New Orleans. I walked up the narrow staircase and entered a room with several bunk beds. I chose a bottom bunk. After settling into our room, Tom and I walked briskly east for two miles on Canal Street to Bourbon Street. Walking always aided in my recovery after cycling for consecutive days. Bourbon Street was just as I had remembered it. When Tara was a baby, Kelley and I stayed at the Royal Sonesta on Bourbon Street during Mardi Gras in 1992. We were in town to attend a company award trip. We walked into the Royal Sonesta lobby. At the registration table, one of the employees handed me an envelope with two hundred dollars inside. A little extra spending money for the three days in New Orleans, compliments of my employer. I thought, "Wow, I like this company!" After serving seven years in the Army and being less than two years into my professional career, two hundred dollars was a big deal.

Katrina devastated New Orleans in 2005, but Bourbon Street looked as I remembered it when I visited in the nineties. The sun shone brightly. Bourbon Street was full of activity. Tom and I sat at a high-top table inside a bar and watched college football. Joel, Tom, and I stayed together for much of the day, checking out all that New Orleans had to offer. When I looked up at Jackson Square, I flashed back to 1985. While stationed at Fort Polk, my folks and youngest brother, Kevin, flew to Louisiana and met me in New Orleans for a planned vacation. Great memories. Joel waited in a lengthy line at Café du Monde for beignets. And then the three of us walked to Pat O'Brien's for that famous hurricane beverage (a mix of light and dark rum, passion fruit, orange and lime juice, simple syrup, and grenadine, and garnished with an orange slice and a cherry). Boy, did that taste great! So refreshing! (That was the only time I consumed alcohol besides the celebration dinner the night before arriving at St. Augustine.)

We had a wonderful excursion in New Orleans on the extra day off the saddle. Back at Perry's Hostel, around a campfire, the group shared stories about our visit to Bourbon Street with Perry and her husband. As much as I enjoyed the extra day off the saddle, I itched to get back on the road. I settled into my tent and quickly fell asleep.

November 5 – Jackson to Franklinton (76 miles)

About ten miles after leaving Perry's Hostel, Tom and I stopped to chat with three men at the side of a country road in an impoverished area. They stood next to an old rusty pickup truck shooting the breeze. A small shack with a front porch in the background caught my attention as I approached them. I saw rotted wood and chipped paint on all sides of the bungalow. One of the men reminded me of Rosey Grier, of NFL football fame. He was huge and looked like he could have been a lineman for the New Orleans Saints. I broke the ice with a quip about the Saints. (The Saints beat the Rams in New Orleans on November 4,

2018, 45–35). We all had a little laugh. They asked if I was traveling with "Bubba's" group.

Bubba's Pampered Pedalers began organizing bike tours all over the United States in 1993. Its founder, Bubba, an avid cyclist and retired police officer, created a unique vacation and bike touring experience. His goal was simple: to "pamper you along the way."[34] Many people I met assumed another one of Bubba's tours was passing through. It was not the first time I'd heard Bubba's name come up in conversation with folks I met on my journey. His approach is different than that of the ACA with its self-contained tour. Bubba's team oversees everything except the cycling. For many people, it's a terrific way to tour long distances. When I decided to ride across the country, I wrangled with how best to approach the challenge. Ultimately, I decided to complete the ride without support. I thought it would be more fulfilling. The way I looked at it, go big or go home. Bubba's approach just was not for me at this juncture.

Random encounters with strangers were the best part of the ride. Here I was in the middle of rural Louisiana having a heartfelt conversation with three African American men: Earl, Orlando, and Raymond. Each one of us was genuinely interested in what the other person had to say. The common thread was cycling, and although the fifteen-minute conversation was brief, I felt like we had much more in common and could have talked for a longer period. I regret not spending more time talking to those three guys. It was one of my favorite pictures, four of us standing side by side, smiling.

About five miles further, I looked to my left and saw a New York Giants flag attached to a pole smack-dab in the middle of a front yard. For a moment, I thought about ringing the doorbell. Brian and I are Giants fans, and I thought it would be cool to introduce myself. I only thought about it for a second, though, because I was not familiar with Louisiana's trespassing laws. I did not want to add my name to the

---

34 bubbaspamperedpedalers.com

trespassers shooting statistic database. It is easy to forget about everything else going on in the world when you're riding a bicycle in the middle of the country. When I passed a "Vote Here" sign on a quiet country road in Franklinton, it dawned on me that it was November 5; election day was tomorrow. I thought about Earl Brown and the judgeship in Shepherd, Texas, and the Senate seat race between Ted Cruz and Beto O'Rourke in Texas and wondered who would win.

The primitive Washington Parish Fair Campsite in Franklinton, Louisiana, our home for the night and our last in Louisiana, was without electricity, running water, bathroom facilities, or cell service. It was not a pleasant night. The wet ground, high humidity, and rampant mosquitos created a difficult environment in which to set up camp and sleep. My legs were unusually sore and out of sync when I arrived at camp. The rolling hills and extra days off the saddle in New Orleans had disrupted my normal routine. My body had become accustomed to riding several hours each day. The extra day off recalibrated my body, so it felt like I was starting over again when I left Perry's Hostel. At our map meeting in Franklinton, Joyce told us that several cross-country touring groups ranked the ride from Jackson, Louisiana, to Franklinton, Louisiana, the most difficult of the entire fifty-seven days on the saddle. It was a tough day for sure, but not the most difficult, in my estimation.

Chapter 6

MISSISSIPPI (BUFFETT, BULL RIDING, AND BBQ)

November 6 – Franklinton to Poplarville (51 miles)

S hortly after crossing the border into Mississippi, I prepared myself to experience the same poverty and uneven roads as in Louisiana. To my pleasant surprise, this was not the case. As soon as I crossed into Mississippi, the landscape shifted. No longer surrounded by trash and rundown buildings, I looked out at green pastures, well-kept houses, and manicured lawns. The roads were clean and nicely paved. Minimal vehicle traffic made up for the nonexistent road shoulders.

Crossing the Mississippi border brought a new sense of excitement. One more state down. Three states to go.

When I checked in at our campsite's registration desk at the Haas-Cienda Ranch RV Park, a large man and a young lady welcomed me to their park. Another guest entered the office and gave me a puzzled look. I did not know if my cycling attire or another reason had triggered the look. He asked, "Where are you from, and where are you going?"

"New Jersey. I'm in a group riding our bicycles across the country," I responded.

"New Jersey?!" he asked as if I was from a foreign country.

Rather than continue discussing the bike ride, I pivoted and chimed in before he could continue. "I used to live in Alabama, Louisiana, Georgia, and Texas. My first time to Mississippi." I wanted to connect myself with the South rather than be seen as a Yankee from the North. I walked out of the office, and that was the last time I saw him. Why I overreacted as I did, I do not know.

After dinner, the group huddled around a table for our map meeting. A park employee stopped by and began talking to us. He asked, "Where are you guys from and where are you going?"

I remember looking at his disfigured head and thinking he must have been in an accident. He told us that he used to be ranked the world's third-best bull rider. It was a very tough way to make a living; his head injury was the result of a bull crushing part of his skull. He was also missing fingers on both hands. He told us his father had instilled in him a never-give-up mentality. Working at the RV park brought him satisfaction. It was work he was still capable of doing well. Everyone has a story. Take an interest, stop, listen, and people will amaze you.

November 7 – Poplarville to Ocean Springs (78 miles)

In the eastern section of the country, towns are much closer together. Since entering Louisiana, I had ridden through towns at a good clip, one after another.

Our destination, The Shed BBQ & Blues Joint, found at a campsite a few miles south of Vancleave, Mississippi, is known to serve the best barbeque. The Shed's story is engrossing. According to theshedbbq.com, the owner, Brad Orrison, decorated the joint with stuff he'd accumulated over the years rummaging through dumpsters on weekends while attending Ole Miss:

And one sobering morning, he surveyed all the junk he'd collected over the years… Not knowing what to do with it and not willing to part with a single plastic bucket or warped wood, he built a trailer out of the larger parts and loaded the rest on top of a homemade junk hauler and moved back to Ocean Springs… One day he had an epiphany: "I'm going to build myself a take-out barbeque joint with all this junk!" Brad (24) and his sister Brooke (19) hammered and nailed… A few weeks after opening, Brad's brother Brett (22), sound engineer for the House of Blues in New Orleans, breezed in with all his knowledge and contacts and set up one of the finest BBQ & Blues venues in the South.[35]

On the night we ate at the Shed, a nasty storm was upon us. We managed to eat without too much rain dripping through the ceiling onto our food inside the Shed. A sign plastered above our table summed up the essence of the Shed philosophy: "Why is the man who invests all your money called a broker?" So out of place, but at the same time, so appropriate.

Shortly before leaving Mississippi, I rode over the Pascagoula River and through Jimmy Buffett's birthplace and hometown, which triggered a memory of the first and only time I attended a Buffett concert, at an open-air venue in San Jose, California, in 1989. My youngest brother, Kevin, who lived with me at the time in Salinas, California, joined me and my Army buddy Carlos for the one-hour drive to San Jose. While I wouldn't consider myself a true fan, or "Parrothead," as his devoted fans are called, I remember having a blast, but not much else because we snuck into the venue with a batch of jello shots. I did, however, send a picture of the "Welcome to the Birthplace of Jimmy Buffett" sign to a former coworker, presumably a self-proclaimed Parrothead, who has traveled over the years far and wide to attend more than 250 Buffett concerts.

---

35 Theshedbbq.com

Chapter 7

ALABAMA (FORREST, FOG, AND FERRY)

November 8 – Ocean Springs to Dauphin Island (61 miles)

While days had become routine, I kept at it, expecting the unexpected. Wake up, pack, eat, ride, set up camp, eat, map meeting, and lights out. Repeat. Repeat. Repeat. I resisted the temptation of going through the motions, riding from town to town, setting my sights on St. Augustine. I wanted to enjoy each day, but I also wanted to finish and see my family. It had been fifty-five days since I'd flown from New Jersey to San Diego. I had taken hundreds of pictures, spoken to hundreds of strangers, and cycled through more than two hundred small towns—all leaving an indelible imprint on my mind. I thought long and hard about not taking the last few days for granted just because I could taste the finish line.

Something felt different about crossing the Alabama state border. Maybe it was because I lived in Alabama many years ago and I connected to when I stepped onto Alabama soil. The largest of all the state border signs, Alabama's was at least twenty feet high and had a nice ring to it:

"Welcome to Sweet Home Alabama." Thoughts of the past—riding on Highway 84 from Fort Rucker near Enterprise, Alabama, through Dothan, Alabama, to Panama City Beach, Florida, for a weekend of fun in the sun with my newly commissioned 2nd lieutenant friends—came alive riding on Highway 614 in Grand Bay, Alabama, on this gloomy, cloudy Thursday morning. I searched my mind for the right visualization, hoping something would trigger a memory. I could not pinpoint why entering Alabama felt different, but it did.

I saw the Gordon Persons Bridge through the dense fog a couple of miles further ahead as I rode along Highway 193 toward the campsite on Dauphin Island, Alabama. From my vantage point, it appeared that the climb toward the top was at a forty-five-degree incline, without railings. I worried about getting blown sideways by the wind at the top. The thought of riding over the bridge concerned me initially, especially with how creepy and eerie the surrounding area looked. There is a reason films have scenes with fog—they lend a creepy effect. The closer I got to the bridge, the less intimidating the climb appeared. It was a very deceiving look from a distance.

As I started my descent toward the opposite shore, I could tell right away I was entering a beach community. There were many condominiums, hotels, and a lot of construction along the coastal highway. Surrounded by water on all sides, I remember thinking I had reached civilization. I thought about the countless family vacations at the Jersey Shore and Outer Banks in North Carolina. I was no longer at risk of being stuck in the middle of the desert and stranded without drinking water. I had a feeling I'd already completed the ride because, at this point, it was just a matter of time before signs for St. Augustine appeared.

The Dauphin Island campground was directly across the street from the ferry that would take us across Mobile Bay to Florida, first thing in the morning. It took me a while to find the campground because I mistakenly turned west instead of east on Bienville Boulevard and rode about three miles out of my way. Realizing my mistake when I reached the end of a paved road on West End Beach, I turned around, annoyed with myself, and retraced my tracks, eventually arriving at the campground. It was my turn to cook and clean again. The closest grocery store was near the Dauphin Island Marina on Highway 193, close to the same place I had entered Dauphin Island! I got on my bike, retraced my tracks two and a half miles, bought dinner items, and then returned to the campground. Extra miles ridden due to a wrong turn or purposely in order to go off the main route were known as "bonus miles." I rode bonus miles on the day I left San Diego, the day I got to Tempe, and the day I arrived on Dauphin Island. I was pleasantly surprised that I had ridden off-course only three cycling days out of fifty-seven.

At the map meeting, I learned that Bayou La Batre, a small fishing village on the Mississippi Sound that I'd ridden through earlier that day, was featured in Tom Hank's famous movie *Forrest Gump*. Gump's Army buddy Bubba Blue and later Gump himself called Bayou La Batre home. I thought back to when I'd crossed a bridge and entered the small fishing village; the stench from rotten fish was so overwhelming that I held my breath and rode as fast as possible to get through the town. That smell was the *worst*.

I am one of the very few who had not seen *Forrest Gump* from start to finish before I began this journey; I had only seen bits and pieces. Before leaving, a couple of friends referred to me as Forrest Gump on a bike. In the middle of Texas, riding on one of those never-ending roads, Joel and I reached the crest of a hill, and we both looked out over the vast valley below with mountains stretched in front as far as the eye could see. Joel broke the silence: "This reminds me of the *Forrest Gump* scene when he stops running and says he's tired and going home." I watched the movie upon returning home. Joel's description of the Texas road was spot-on.

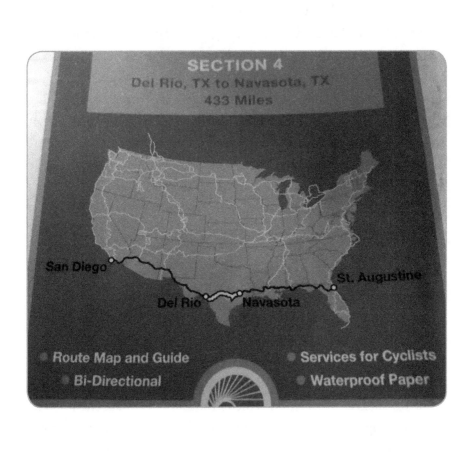

SECTION 4
Del Río, TX to Navasota, TX
433 Miles

San Diego

St. Augustine

Del Río   Navasota

Route Map and Guide   Services for Cyclists

Bi-Directional   Waterproof Paper

Oct. 16, 2018 – Klaus, Joel, Tom, Joyce, Wally and Larry at dinner in Uvalde, Texas

Oct. 17, 2018 – Klaus, Tom and Larry at the Lost Maples
State Natural Area, Real County, Texas

Oct. 17, 2018 – Drying clothes inside bathroom at the Lost Maples State Natural Area

Oct. 18, 2018 – Meeting cowboys at the General Store in Hunt, Texas

Oct. 21, 2018 – Crossing Flat Creek on the way to Austin, Texas

Oct. 23, 2018 – Flooded Colorado River, Bastrop KOA, Bastrop, Texas

Oct. 24, 2018 – "Who wore it best?", Larry, Wally or Tom—
before leaving the KOA in Bastrop, Texas

Oct. 24, 2018 – First Longhorn sighting, Smithville, Texas

Oct. 24, 2018 – Joel and Larry avoiding
the rain in La Grange, Texas

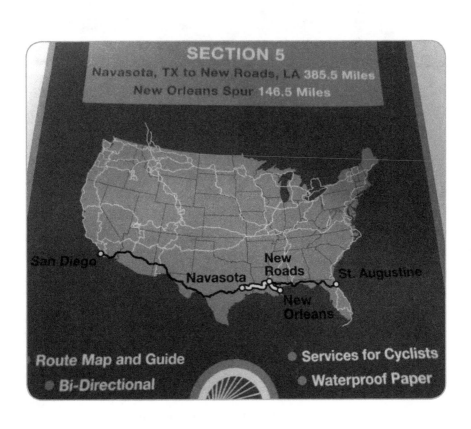

SECTION 5

Navasota, TX to New Roads, LA 385.5 Miles

New Orleans Spur 146.5 Miles

San Diego

Navasota

New Roads

New Orleans

St. Augustine

Route Map and Guide

Services for Cyclists

Bi-Directional

Waterproof Paper

Oct. 26, 2018 – Larry, Joel and Travis at the Cagle
Recreation Area campground, New Waverly, Texas

Oct. 31, 2018 – Krazy Cajun Café, Mamou, Louisiana

Oct. 31, 2018 – Travis shopping on Halloween in Ville Platte, Louisiana

Nov. 5, 2018 – Catching up with the locals, Denham Springs, Louisiana

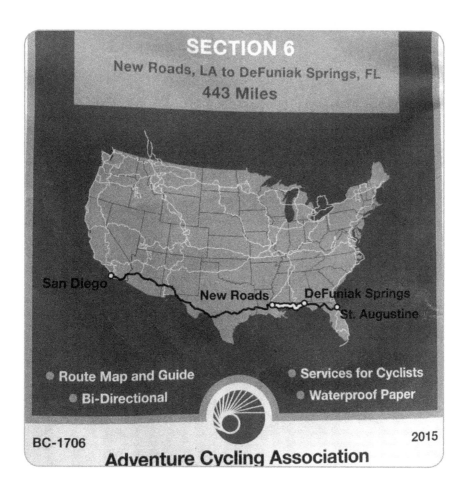

SECTION 6

New Roads, LA to DeFuniak Springs, FL

443 Miles

San Diego

New Roads

DeFuniak Springs

St. Augustine

● Route Map and Guide   ● Services for Cyclists

● Bi-Directional   ● Waterproof Paper

BC-1706

2015

Adventure Cycling Association

Nov. 6, 2018
Louisiana and
Mississippi border near
Poplarville, Mississippi

Nov. 7, 2018 – The Shed in Vancleave, Mississippi

Nov. 8, 2018 – Jimmy Buffett's birthplace, Pascagoula, Mississippi

SECTION 7

DeFuniak Springs, FL to St. Augustine, FL

409.5 Miles

San Diego

DeFuniak Springs

St. Augustine

- Route Map and Guide
- Bi-Directional
- Services for Cyclists
- Waterproof Paper

BC-1707

Nov. 8, 2018
Mississippi and Alabama
border crossing near
Grand Bay, Alabama

Nov. 9, 2018 – Ferry ride across Mobile Bay from
Dauphin Island to Fort Morgan, Alabama

Nov. 10, 2018 – Blue Angel Fighter jets on display:
National Naval Aviation Museum, Pensacola, Florida

Nov. 12, 2018
Departing Black River State
Park, a few sizes too small,
Santa Rosa County, Florida

Nov. 14, 2018 – Effects of Hurricane Michael on Highway 90 near Marianna, Florida

Nov. 14, 2018 – Effects of Hurricane Michael on Highway 90 near Marianna, Florida

*Nov. 16, 2018 – Doug, Joel, and Travis relaxing before dinner at
Suwannee River State Park, Suwannee County, Florida*

*Nov. 17, 2018 – Klaus preparing dinner at Ichetucknee
Springs State Park, near Fort White, Florida*

Nov. 19, 2018
Doug and Larry enjoying
a cold one at Musselwhite's
Seafood & Grill in East
Palatka, Florida

Nov. 20, 2018
Official finish line downtown
St. Augustine, Florida

Nov. 20, 2018
Jeff and Kris welcome
me to the finish in St.
Augustine, Florida

Nov. 20, 2018 – Dipping tire in the Atlantic Ocean on Anastasia Island, Florida

Chapter 8

FLORIDA (DETOUR, DEBRIS, AND DONE!)

November 9 – Dauphin Island to Pensacola (56 miles)

By 7:30 a.m., we all had checked in at the ferry and waited to board for the short twenty-minute ride across Mobile Bay. Oil rigs in the distance stuck out of the bay like ugly eyesores. We all leaned our bikes against the side of the ferry platform, looked out over the boat toward the horizon, and soaked in the early morning breeze under hazy skies. Travis asked a ferry passenger to take a picture of the group smiling and standing side by side, each wearing a different bright and colorful jersey, framed against the soupy morning sky. The group picture is one of my favorites. Eight riders looked and felt like they were on top of the world. We had been together for many weeks and formed close bonds. We all appreciated making it this far, and I am sure we wished the ferry ride could have been much longer.

For part of the ferry ride, we each stood alone, gazing out into the bay. I wondered what went through everyone's mind. Were they ready for the ride to be over? Did they regret having come on the journey? Did they feel like I did, that the trip surpassed their wildest expectations?

The temperature dropped into the sixties and would fall into the thirties in a couple of days. Real estate signs dominated the coastline from the time we got off the ferry at Fort Morgan and all along the Alabama Gulf Coast's thirty-two miles of sugar-white-sand beaches. The signs stopped when we reached a roadside sign that read "Gulf Shores, a small-town community with big wide-open beaches." I could not believe how much undeveloped land existed in this section of the Alabama panhandle. I wondered why. It seemed like prime real estate to me. Why wasn't this area built up like so much else along the Florida Panhandle?

The night before we arrived in the Gulf Shores area, Kelley's cousin Mike had graciously offered to let us spend the night at his home close to Gulf Shores. But we had already made arrangements to stay at the First United Methodist Church's Youth Ministries Building in downtown Pensacola.

I had a huge feeling of personal satisfaction when I crossed into Florida. Klaus and I arrived at the border sign at the same time. Tom was not too far behind. We all stopped for a few minutes to take pictures. I was a little careless, and, in my enthusiasm, I caught my shoe cleat in the pedal when hopping off Tank. I lost my balance and fell onto my butt. Luckily, I have a lot of padding back there, so I did not injure myself. I stayed on the ground laughing for a minute, not realizing part of my body was on the road. A car approached and Tom yelled, "Get off the road!" I quickly did. I gathered myself, and before continuing to Pensacola, I thought, "Larry, now is not the time to be careless; you are so close to the end. You need to say focused."

November 10 – Pensacola (Rest Day)

I am not sure why the group referred to days off the saddle as rest days. They were anything but rest for me. I woke up early to a sunny, thirty-five-degree cold and quiet morning; I decided to walk around before others arose. I saw more churches per square mile than in Texas, Mississippi, and Louisiana combined. There were many monuments throughout the city, highlighting the historical elements of its past. Pensacola was inhabited by Native American people before Spanish explorers' arrival in the sixteenth century. Pensacola changed hands often among different Western powers, including Spain, France, and England. The Battle of Pensacola was fought in 1861. During the Civil War, the Confederates kept control of the city for several months after the battle ended. Monuments to the American Revolution are also on display, including one commemorating the Siege of Pensacola, the most prolonged battle of the American Revolution.

As I walked through downtown, I thought about the destruction Hurricane Katrina caused here. Today, the town seems rebuilt and full of activity, though it's only one storm away from utter devastation and the upending of lives once again. In the back of my mind, I do wonder what it's like to live in the coastal communities along the Florida Panhandle every year when hurricane season rolls around.

Today's surprise would once again prompt me to reflect on the great country in which we live. It would bring a little levity as well. Tom and I hailed an Uber driver for a late afternoon visit to the National Naval Aviation Museum on the outskirts of downtown Pensacola. About halfway to the museum, the Uber driver (from Haiti and still learning the language) told us he felt blessed because today was his first day on the job and we were his first customers. He was working to put himself through school.

We approached the guard gate. The driver rolled down the window to show his identification. Because of the language barrier, I volunteered to the guard, "I called Uber for a ride to the museum."

The guard said, "No, no, no, Ubers are not allowed. It is a crime for Uber to enter, subject to a five-hundred-dollar fine and up to one year in prison." I interrupted and told the guard it was my fault because we were from out of town and unaware of the rules. The guard gave the driver a warning and signaled us to turn the car around so we could leave.

We all took a breath. I asked the driver, "Do you still feel blessed?" We all laughed it off. Tom and I hailed a taxi that was preapproved to enter the base. We arrived about an hour before closing. The pressure was on once we entered the museum—so much to see in less than an hour.

I found the two displays I was specifically hoping to see. A couple of my former coworkers were naval aviators. They'd told me their separate units were on display, one from the early 1980s and another from the 1991 Gulf War. I tracked down USS Ranger, CVW-9, known as the "screw birds" and the second unit, Helicopter Combat Support Squadron (HCS) 4 and 5 from Operation Iraqi Freedom, 2003–2004 (National Naval Aviation Museum, November 10, 2018). I sent texts to both of my friends, letting them know they were famous!

Another highlight for me was seeing the Blue Angels F/A-18 Hornet fighter jet up close. Smack-dab in the middle of the main museum building, three life-sized jets hung from the rafters, an example of the awesome firepower of the United States military. A museum employee announced over the loudspeaker that we had five minutes until closing. It was time to return to the church and prepare for the next day. While the days blended more and more, each day also brought surprises, twists and turns that I could never have scripted. There was not a dull moment on the trip.

The trip had been everything I hoped it would be and more. I often told people the reason I was doing this was that I wanted a physical and mental challenge. But there was more. I did not know how to define "more," but I knew I wanted something else. I had plenty of time to reflect and not have to worry about anything else. My mind was free. I spoke to Kelley on most days. I texted with family members and occasionally with friends. In total, I watched a little over an hour of TV in the space of two months. I did not take one phone call from anyone except a family member.

I wanted to experience the unknown, meet new people, and learn about different American cultures on my ride. I was living my life the way I wanted to live it. I did not only wonder and ponder; I took action and am thankful I did. I would not have served in the Army without taking action (and encouragement from my parents). I would not have served in Korea without taking it upon myself and proactively requesting a new assignment. There would have been no Ranger, Airborne, Infantry training without acting, no serving my country during a hostile conflict without acting, no living in fourteen states without acting, and no meeting Kelley and raising a fantastic family without acting. And the possibility of stumbling upon a new career, a new passion after returning home if the ride triggered something I had not contemplated before. All possible because I did more than contemplate. I acted.

November 11 and 12 – Pensacola to Blackwater River State Park (43 miles) and Blackwater River State Park to DeFuniak Springs (49 miles)

Rather than continue due east from Pensacola toward Panama City, which was the planned route, we rode north/northeast to avoid the Florida coastline devastated by Hurricane Michael that had touched down a month before our arrival. The storm completely wiped out many of the campsites along the primary route. We camped at Blackwater River State Park, far north of the significant destruction. The temperature continued to hover around thirty-five to forty degrees. There was a greater than 50 percent chance of rain for the next couple of days. The days grew shorter as we crossed the Apalachicola River and entered the eastern time zone. Tree canopies also reduced ambient light on Florida roads and campsites.

The group strung a line from tree to tree and hung a few lights to hold our map meeting. It was pitch black at 6:30 p.m. I entered my tent around 7:00 and settled in for a long night. At 3:00 a.m. it started to rain, and by 5:30, the skies opened. My Big Agnes tent worked like a charm; inside, I was dry and cozy. Outside the tent was a different story. It was raining buckets. I hopped out of my tent, knowing I would get soaked, and ran to the bathroom building. Others in the group arrived, and we all congregated underneath the covered porch area just outside the bathrooms. We decided to eat breakfast there under the overhang.

We had no choice but to start pedaling toward our next destination. I donned indispensable cold and wet weather gear, including a colorful red rain jacket, black pants, gloves, and overshoes, and I added a bright yellow rain cover to my helmet. Amid miserable weather, we all experienced a lighthearted moment when I evoked a burst of collective and cheerful group laughter.

"Hey Larry, look up," Travis said, as everyone stopped what they were doing and, in unison, all began laughing. Little did I realize I resembled a cartoon character with a small yellow helmet perched at an angle on top of my red rain jacket cover. I appeared to be wearing a helmet that was four sizes too small on top of another helmet. I looked very silly. It was a light moment to help kick off a particularly challenging day on the saddle.

I could deal with horrible cycling weather if a dry room awaited me. But today, I rode through relentless downpours the entire day on my way to the Sunset King Lake RV Resort near DeFuniak Springs, Florida, and there I would spend another night in a tent exposed to the outside elements. I stopped at gas stations and convenience stores often to dry off throughout the day. I met kind folks each time I stopped to rest. I was called "sweetie" more times than I can remember.

The last time I was in this area of Florida was November 1988. When I looked at the map the night before, I realized I would cycle by Eglin Air Force Base (AFB) in the morning. I began reliving the nightmare of the time I spent at Eglin AFB going through the swamp phase of Ranger School.

The circuitous journey to Ranger School started in Korea when I connected with Mr. Fish and requested to attend the Infantry Officer Advanced Course (IOAC) and Ranger School instead of the Air Defense Artillery Officer Advanced Course, which would be the usual path. (This was the same Mr. Fish at the Pentagon who had honored my request to go to Korea the year before.) When I received permanent change of station (PCS) transfer orders to Fort Benning, Georgia, I was ecstatic and surprised. Ranger School assignments are mostly allotted to career infantry officers, not my branch, Air Defense Artillery. In March 1988, I boarded a plane, destination Fort Benning, Georgia. IOAC is a four-month training school for infantry officers to develop leadership skills needed for a company-size command assignment (a company has between one hundred and two hundred soldiers). Ranger School is a two-month small-unit tactic and leadership course "that develops functional skills directly related to units whose mission is to engage the enemy in close combat and direct fire battle."[36] Ranger School is one of the most challenging military training courses. The third phase of ranger training, swamp phase, takes place at Eglin AFB. It was, by far, the most difficult phase for me. I prepared for Ranger School for more than a year. Back then, I was in the best physical shape of my life. I could easily knock out a hundred push-ups and sit-ups in perfect form. I could run two miles in combat boots in less than twelve minutes. I was ready to go.

The first phase of Ranger School took place in Fort Benning. The ranger assessment phase evaluated physical fitness and basic infantry skills and included a stressful land navigation test. Training usually started at four in the morning and lasted well into the night. I walked briskly (and jogged) for several kilometers through thick, high brush, swamps, and marshes, looking for predetermined points in the woods. Each ranger student had five hours to find a specific number of eight-digit grid coordinates using paper maps; otherwise, they failed. I remember holding one hand in front of my face so I would not poke out an eye while navigating through the brush in the dark (a ranger student was medevacked while patrolling during the swamp phase, when brush snapped and penetrated directly into his eye). By the time phase one was over, close to 50 percent of the students did not make it to the second phase. I passed phase one, but not without pushing myself to the limit.

---

36 Benning.army.mil.ranger

I slept the entire three-hour bus ride from Fort Benning to Dahlonega, Georgia, the location for phase two, the mountain phase. In that phase, I learned Australian rappelling (descending a fixed rope in a standing position while facing the ground). I also learned how to rappel out of a helicopter and did my best not to give ranger instructors a reason to send me home. My memories were not all bad ones, especially eating blueberry pancakes for breakfast at the chow hall.

I was halfway to earning the coveted ranger tab after successfully completing the mountain phase. That all came to a screeching halt about halfway through phase three, the swamp phase at Eglin AFB. All I remember is waking up at about three in the morning to shouts of "Ranger Walsh! Ranger Walsh!" (Ranger instructors refer to all students by "Ranger–last name.") I had slept through an op-order meeting (operation order meeting) starting at 3:00 a.m. for a mission where I held a squad leadership role. Because I did not make the meeting on time, I failed the mission and the phase. Before I was flown back to Fort Benning on a UH-1 Huey helicopter to begin my recycle phase, I was summoned to the office of the Ranger School battalion commander, who in no uncertain terms told me I was a "pathetic excuse for a soldier."

I was demoralized. I had been in the service for four years and contemplated making the military a career. I remember thinking that plan was no longer a possibility. I did not know what to expect at Fort Benning. After a few days of cleaning latrines and pondering my future, I was instructed by the Fort Benning Ranger School commander to gather my belongings; I was being flown back to Eglin AFB for a chance to continue with the next ranger class. I was relieved. I had another opportunity to prove myself.

I loaded up my rucksack and jumped inside the Huey helicopter for the two-hundred-mile flight south to Eglin Air Force Base. Several weeks later, after completing the swamp phase and the last step, the desert phase at the Dugway Proving Ground in Utah, I graduated from Ranger School. (Today, Ranger School consists of three phases of training: Fort Benning hosts the assessment phase, Dahlonega the mountain phase, and Eglin Air Force Base the swamp phase). I was immensely proud to have earned the ranger tab. And, thrilled, my father traveled to Fort Benning to attend my graduation ceremony.

Completing ranger training was a new goal after entering the Army as a 2nd lieutenant. I have proudly carried my tab since 1988. It is with me wherever I go.

November 13 – DeFuniak Springs to Marianna (71 miles)

Many memories were running through my mind as I rode my bike along Highway 90 on my way to Marianna, Florida. The phrase "embracing the suck" came to mind as I continued my journey east. I experienced the second day of unrelenting rain. The rain and cold temperatures put a damper on what otherwise would have been an enjoyable ride on the nicely paved Florida roads. Wasn't this the Sunshine State? It sure did not feel like it.

On Highway 90, I saw the effects of Hurricane Michael. My location was about fifty miles due north of Panama City, where the hurricane had touched down a month before. The pictures I took did not do justice to the damage I saw. The storm chopped trees in half. Blue tarps still served as makeshift roofs for many buildings and many businesses that remained closed. The twisted metal was strewn all over, in some places still clinging to trees. A gas station structure was ripped from its foundation. Schools finally opened after being closed for over a month.

Memories of my young adult life continued as I made my way across the Florida Panhandle. Military jargon is foreign to civilians. So are military careers. But suffice it to say that my path was not typical. Six months before that fateful meeting in October 1984 with MG Leuer at Fort Polk, Louisiana, I was selected into the Military Intelligence branch of the US Army, only to be reassigned into the newly formed Army Aviation branch, and then reassigned once again into the Air Defense Artillery branch. Between April 9 and August 10, 1984, a matter of 123 days, Uncle Sam placed me into three branches of the US Army: Military Intelligence, Aviation, and Air Defense Artillery, the branch I served in for seven years. My Army career is distinguished by a uniquely nontraditional path—emblematic, and a foreshadowing of the next thirty-four years.

When I received orders to attend the Army Aviation Officer Basic Training at Fort Rucker, Alabama, I was excited beyond belief. The basic leadership officer training was scheduled to begin in June 1984, and the flight training part (twenty-week Rotary Wing Aviator Course) in December 1984. On May 20, 1984, I graduated from college and was commissioned a 2nd lieutenant in Army Aviation. Less than two weeks later, I drove to Enterprise, Alabama, home of Fort Rucker, to learn to fly helicopters! I was issued an olive drab flight suit with my name tag: "2nd LT Lawrence Walsh." I could not wait to start training, a proud 2nd lieutenant entering one of the first Army Aviation officer training schools since Congress had created the branch the year before.

The Officers Club on Fort Rucker was the place to be on Friday nights. Think *Top Gun*, but replace F-14 Tomcat jets with UH-1 Army helicopters. It was much less of an ordeal for civilians to enter military bases in the 1980s than it is today. One Friday evening at the Officers Club, a girl approached me. She asked if I was a pilot. "Not yet. But I'm starting flight school in a couple of weeks." I still remember the look on her face. She wanted to meet someone who already had their wings.

My time at Fort Rucker was cut short. I did not pass an eye exam needed for all students before starting the Aviation Officer Basic School, an eye exam I had passed once before, in the summer of 1983 when I attended training at Fort Bragg, North Carolina. My depth perception was not standard. Whether I failed the stereopsis test or something else, I am not sure; it was a word I had never heard before. All I remember is hearing the news that I could not continue in the Aviation branch. The branch placement officer gave me three other branches to choose from: Armor, Field Artillery, and Air Defense Artillery. I did not fit in an M60 tank; therefore, Armor was not seriously considered. I flipped a coin, and that is how I ended up at Fort Bliss in El Paso, Texas, home of Air Defense Artillery. So much for Fort Rucker.

Dozens of memories filled my mind, distracting my attention from the miserable weather. I stopped at a Dollar General store to get out of the unrelenting rain and shop for dinner. Doug, Travis, Joel, and Klaus soon arrived. When we'd left the campsite earlier that morning, we all understood that cooking under the stars was the plan for when we arrived at the motel in Marianna. Travis and Doug congregated outside the store underneath the narrow overhang away from the rain. They expressed their desire to eat at a restaurant. They had previously texted the group explaining that their dinner plans had changed and not to count them in for outside cooking. Anyone interested in joining them at a restaurant should let them know.

After leaving the Dollar General store, I discerned a difference in thinking between members of the group, some of whom had not weighed in on the earlier group text message. This was the first time dinner plans had changed in the middle of the day. It would have been miserable to cook outside, for sure. I had been somewhat oblivious to a friction developing among some group members. Trust, healthy conflict, and commitment to agreed-upon plans—all elements of an effective team— had remained solid through both the good and the tough riding days. A genuine feeling of goodwill toward each other was exhibited from San Diego to Florida. But now, with less than a week to go, a chasm grew. I had made a conscious decision in San Diego that I would supply the antidote to any negativity that crept into the group dynamics. Attitude is the one thing I knew I had control over. In hindsight, upon reflection, problems started bubbling to the surface in Palo Verde, California, as we rode through the Imperial Sand Dunes. Riding in extreme weather conditions was the trigger that began the conflict.

Several miles of riding remained after I left the Dollar General store. The relentless downpour subsided. I looked up while pedaling east on Highway 90, and in the distance I saw smoke billowing about three hundred yards ahead. At first, I thought it was a controlled burn, but as I got closer, I realized the smoke was coming from cars that had been involved in a crash. I stopped short of the collision, about twenty-five yards away, placed my bike on the ground, and jogged up to the scene to assess the situation.

A young adult female was inside the car on the driver's side. Someone was trying to unfasten the seat belt and separate her from the car. An older woman, maybe thirty, held a small child in her arms and stood about twenty feet away from the collision. The crying child looked to be around two years old but did not appear to be injured. I ran back to my bike and retrieved two Smartwool sweaters that I carried in one of my panniers. I ran to the woman holding the child and placed the sweaters around the child's body. No one panicked, but no one had thought about covering the child with warm clothing.

One of the firefighters who came upon the crash scene—David from Chipley, Florida—told me his heart stopped when he saw my bike on the ground. He thought the accident involved a cyclist, due to my bike's proximity to the crash scene. He was relieved I was not in the accident. David told me that five years earlier, in 2013, he had been hit by a car when riding his bike on a road in California. He had only recently fully recovered to where he could manage the physical activity associated with his work as an emergency medical technician. It was a sobering moment.

About an hour after arriving at the crash scene, an ambulance left with the child and the driver. The injuries did not appear to be serious. David gave me his contact information and asked me to send him a note (which I did) when I was safely back home in New Jersey. I was thankful to have been on the scene so quickly and able to supply warm clothing for the child.

Late that afternoon I entered the town of Marianna and checked in to the motel. Joyce called a meeting in the lobby to discuss dinner plans. After everyone arrived and sat down, the meeting began with a few riders expressing frustration, sharing an example of something that had occurred days earlier. The topic triggered a discussion that I could tell was going to lead to more quarreling. To me, the criticism seemed misplaced. I felt it was not the time or the place to raise grievances. A private discussion would be a better approach. It became clear that frustrations had been building for some time. I interrupted and made my opinion known, telling the group I would not be part of the debate.

"Come on, guys," I said. "We're one week away from completing this incredible journey. Let's focus on the big picture—the Atlantic Ocean!" Here we were, one week away from completing a fantastic cross-country journey, and the conversation had devolved into petty B.S. I excused myself and walked about a mile to a Popeyes Restaurant, treating myself to an eight-piece chicken dinner. It's a decision I regret, but I was angry and needed to remove myself from the situation to settle down. When I returned to the motel later that night, Joyce called me. I shared with her that I was focused on one thing, completing this ride, and nothing was getting in the way of that. I do not know what happened to the dinner items we'd purchased at Dollar General earlier in the day.

About four hundred miles before we arrived at the Atlantic Ocean, my right knee started to bother me. I had a sharp pain at the tip of my right kneecap. Both of my knees had been sore at the beginning of the trip, riding through California. But for the better part of 2,000-plus miles, my joints, including knees, did not cause many problems. I thought the constant rain and cold temperature had started to take a toll on my body.

Overall, my body powered through the rigors of riding long distances each day for weeks at a time. I fully expected my legs to manage the wear and tear of a long bicycle ride. And they did. My lower back, neck, and arms also coped well with the grind of each day on the saddle. My hands and feet bore the brunt of constant pressure, resulting in numbness in my hands and feet and extreme pain, mostly in my right foot. Most surprising, the penile numbness that can occur due to constant pressure on the pudendal artery was not a significant problem for me.[37] On occasion, I stopped to shake my hands, rest my feet, or remove myself

---

37 www.healthline.com/health/numb-penis

from the saddle. And I took four hundred milligrams of Motrin each morning, beginning in Florida. The Motrin alleviated the soreness enough so I could continue riding.

November 14 – Marianna to Tallahassee (71 miles)

Hurricane Michael's devastating impact was felt for close to two hundred miles, from just east of Blackwater River State Park to Tallahassee's western end. The hurricane hit land as a Category 5 in Panama City and kept Category 3 status when it came through Marianna fifty-five miles north of Panama City. Small communities appeared to be empty except for power line workers and roofers. I spoke to a couple of power line workers at the motel in Marianna who were deployed from out of state to help bring the communities back from ruin.

I should have been more excited than I was when I saw a sign welcoming me to Tallahassee. If anything, I was amused to be riding on Tennessee Avenue about to enter Florida State University's campus. The anticipation and excitement of achieving another milestone were replaced with indifference. With about 250 miles to go, I was ready to complete the ride and return home. I forced myself to visit the FSU campus and get a glimpse of Doak Campbell Stadium, home to FSU Seminole football, before checking into the Econo Lodge on Apalachee Parkway, southeast of downtown Tallahassee.

My bike was a dirty mess from riding in the rain for the past few days. The first thing I did was get in line behind Travis to clean my bike using a garden hose attached to a water spigot in the motel parking lot. Dirt was caked on the underbelly, and the gears were full of grease and grime.

November 15 – Tallahassee (Rest Day)

It was our last rest day of the trip. The temperature was in the forties, clouds were out, and rain was in the forecast. This was the only rest day I chose not to explore and take in the surrounding area. I walked to a Sears department store and bought a sweatshirt to replace the wool sweaters I'd given away a couple of days earlier. I joined Wally, Tom, Joyce, and Joel for dinner at a nearby Mexican restaurant, walked back to the motel and, finally, prepared my bike for the ride in the morning.

November 16 – Tallahassee to Suwannee River State Park (76 miles)

I was content leaving Tallahassee, knowing my next rest break would be after dipping my tire in the Atlantic Ocean. The tree canopy prevented direct sunlight from supplying any warmth on this thirty-five-degree early-morning ride toward Gainesville. I stopped in the village of Capitola, Florida, for a cup of hot chocolate.

Capitola, California, on the Central Coast, north of Monterey, is where I met Kelley in May 1991. She claims I do not remember the moment when we first met. I do. She was standing near a keg on the patio of the ground floor condominium that she and several girlfriends had rented for the weekend to celebrate her friend Susie's birthday.

In 2017, Kelley and our three kids visited California for a twenty-fifth-anniversary party. About thirty friends joined us for a celebration in Aptos, California. There was live music, dancing, and a lot of fun had by all who attended. It was hosted by Kelley's good friend Nancy, the same friend who thought I should tackle this ride. We took the kids to all the places Kelley and I had visited when we were dating. Capitola looked the same as I remembered. Great memories and a lot of fun for our family to be together for a few days.

November 17 – Suwannee River State Park to Ichetucknee Springs State Park (57 miles)

When I arrived at Ichetucknee Springs State Park, reality set in—I was close to the Atlantic Ocean. It would be our last night cooking dinner outside and building a campfire to take the edge off the thirty-degree temperature. Everyone seemed relaxed, enjoying one of the last remaining nights on this incredible journey. We met a guy from Jacksonville at the campground. He was walking across the country. He expected to arrive in San Diego about twelve months after starting his journey in Jacksonville, Florida. His feet were swollen from walking so much, so he decided to spend a couple of extra days off his feet, hoping the swelling would go down. I wondered what his motivation was to take on such an extreme journey. Was he also searching for his Yellow Brick Road?

November 18 – Ichetucknee Springs State Park to Gainesville (53 miles)

My ride on Elim Church Road to Highway 441 south on the way to Gainesville was one of the best riding days of the entire trip. The sun shone brightly, and the temperature hovered in the mid-seventies; the recently paved flat roads and the broad road shoulders free of debris combined to form the perfect riding conditions. It hit me when I rode over Interstate 75: we were getting close to the finish!

After entering Gainesville and before arriving at the campsite, I visited the University of Florida campus. In front of the football stadium, I saw a player walking into the stadium for a late Sunday afternoon team meeting. I hollered, "Hello!" trying to begin a conversation. He turned toward me, but he quickened his pace and soon disappeared into the building. He had better things to do than talk to me.

I had another surprise and humorous encounter on the Gainesville-Hawthorne State Trail. A cyclist out for a Sunday ride asked if he could borrow my bike pump. I said, "Sure, but I don't know if it works." I was not joking. Here I was 3,000 miles into a 3,100-mile bike ride, and I had yet to use my bike pump a single time. I was so surprised that I did not have one flat tire on the entire trip. Everyone else had at least one flat, some had multiple flats, and one person had seven flat tires!

The group camped in the backyard of a Warmshowers host in Gainesville. The Warmshowers community is made up of individuals who offer their property to cyclists to shower and camp, and they often serve dinner and breakfast. It's a way to give back to the cycling community that rides through your town.

I set up my tent in the backyard of our host's property next to a small pond. This couple bought their property knowing they lived in an area prone to sinkholes. Over time, a sinkhole filled with water to form the pond. Alligators used to live close by but were no longer present because the food source was gone. Some owners survey their property before buying to figure out whether the land was susceptible to sinkholes. According to our hosts, the problem with surveying is that it can weaken the ground and potentially create more problems. These owners decided to pass on the survey and build their home anyway.

The entire area surrounding Gainesville is susceptible to sinkholes. Most of the state is underlain with water-soluble limestone. Acidic rain mixes with alkaline limestone, creating ground weakness. Rain seeps down into the rocks and dissolves the minerals, leaving cracks and ultimately causing sinkholes.[38] I remembered reading a story in which a bedroom inside a ranch-style home collapsed into the earth. I do not believe the victim, who was sleeping at the time, has ever been found. It is frightening to think that you can disappear into the earth without warning.

November 19 – Gainesville to Palatka (55 miles)

The Quality Inn in Palatka along the St. Johns River was our last destination before the ride to St. Augustine. I had my sights set on a ribeye steak and a nice cold Budweiser. We all knew that within a matter of hours, our time together was coming to an end. Before we took a taxi to the restaurant for our celebration dinner, we sat in the Quality Inn lobby and discussed our plans for transporting our bikes home. Some talked about their flight plans departing from Jacksonville Airport. I planned to send my bike, using the same BikeFlights service,

---

38 www.sinkholemaps.com/blog/what-causes-sinkholes-in-florida

to Whippany Cycle in New Jersey from Sprockets Bicycle Shop in St. Augustine. I would then spend the night at a Marriott next to Interstate 95, a few miles west of St. Augustine. The following morning a taxi would take me to the airport for my flight home to New Jersey.

At our celebration dinner on November 19, 2018, we planned the details of our final day together. At 2:00 p.m. on November 20, we were to rendezvous at the official finish line (intersection of King and Avenida Mendoza) in downtown St. Augustine, capped by a ride over the Bridge of Lions leading to the Atlantic Ocean, for the ceremonial dipping of the tire in the ocean.

And then it would be over.

The dinner was a joyous occasion. But I sensed everyone was relieved to be close to the finish. We talked about taking pictures at the ocean, wanting to capture the end of the journey, to memorialize it for posterity's sake. Doug spouted off that he only planned to stay at the surf for fifteen minutes. I was a little annoyed, but I just let it go. Everyone was ready to return to their real life and regular routine with family and friends. Doug and Travis made plans to connect post-ride. Joyce and Wally would continue their duties as members of the ACA executive committee. I did not make any definite plans to connect with anyone, although we all shared contact information. We bonded as a group as best we could to complete the mission. I thought about Thanksgiving dinner, sitting around the dining room table with my family, relaxing. Finally, a few months removed from a feeling of despair, I had rallied and discovered my Yellow Brick Road.

I was grateful to be present with everyone at Musselwhite's Seafood & Grill in East Palatka, just over the Memorial Bridge. All of us crammed into a single booth, all smiles. Doug was wearing a full whitish-grey beard, the result of sixty-seven days of not shaving. Tom was smiling with his long auburn hair hanging down, no ponytail tonight. He finally let his guard down, and his hair as well. A sense of relief came over all of us. We had made it almost to the end. Some were more tanned than others. All were thinner and healthy-looking. Doug and Klaus were wearing ball caps. Travis was wearing a knit beanie. We all raised a glass to toast a job well done.

After dinner, we took a taxi back to the motel on the west side of Memorial Bridge. Before calling it a night, I walked around Palatka, thinking about the past few months. It was eerily quiet. I walked on St. Johns Avenue, a quiet side street that ran parallel to Reid Street / Highway 17, where the Quality Inn was located. I wanted to be alone and think about life. I stopped at a Dairy Queen and smiled when I thought about the first time we all ate ice cream together at a Dairy Queen in Quartzsite, Arizona, several weeks earlier. We were eleven strong then. Eight still riding now. I was melancholy, reflecting on the intense rush I had experienced in the past nine weeks, knowing I would soon re-enter the world that I had emotionally detached from for three months.

I was a little anxious, not knowing any more than before I left San Diego what I wanted to do professionally for my next chapter in life. I had not had that "aha" moment or any great epiphanies along the way. It was not until I wrote this book that I realized the true impact of riding the Southern Tier. Pedaling my bike from state to state, leapfrogging from time zone to time zone, allowed me to unknowingly reclaim the person I wanted to be, the one I used to be.

November 20 – Palatka to St. Augustine (35 miles)

The distance from Palatka to St. Augustine is thirty-five miles. Before leaving the motel, I walked to Joyce's room and handed her a check. It was a small token of my appreciation for the leadership she provided to all of us. But when I went to her room, knocked on the door, and said, "Good morning Joyce," I had a lump in my throat. I wanted to say more but ended up just saying thank you and walking away. I did not want her to see tears falling from my eyes.

I started the morning ride in rain, wind, and temperatures in the mid-forties. I wanted to show off my new bright and colorful Southern

Tier cycling shirt, so I decided to forgo rain gear. It was a fitting end to a fantastic time on the road with rain to start the day and nice weather to end the ride. All the elements were captured in one short thirty-five-mile ride (except the hills). I took my time. I was not in a rush. I rode alone. I wanted to be free to think. But I did not think. I just rode.

Making it to St. Augustine was surreal. The "Welcome to St. Augustine" sign brought a sense of gratification. I stopped in front of the sign and looked at it. I was happy but also numb. I did not know what to think. It was cool to be there, but I also had a vague sense of letdown. The emotions I felt were much different than the exuberance I experience winning a competitive basketball game. My team is winning by one, the clock runs out, and we all jump, elated to have pulled out a hard-fought game. This was different. I knew completing this journey was a huge milestone, and I was happy to have arrived in St. Augustine. But I also knew I would soon transition back to the real world. I thought about the past few months, my journey from New Jersey to San Diego to St. Augustine. And now it was time to go back home.

At two o'clock, I met up with other riders at the intersection of King and Avenida Mendoza. Within minutes, each of us arrived at the intersection across from a small park near the center of town.

It was my first time visiting St. Augustine, but I did not explore because we still had about five miles to go before seeing the Atlantic Ocean. A welcome surprise appeared: I turned around and saw my friend Jeff and his wife Kris walk up to greet me. I had not seen Jeff in well over a year. The last time was when both he and Kris showed up at my daughter Jaclyn's high school basketball game when she was a senior and they were still living in New Jersey. During our embrace, I could sense he appreciated the closure of my journey, having completed a similar epic trip—a walk through the Appalachian Trail the year before. When we first saw each other, Jeff looked down and said, "Boy, your legs are huge!" Funny, because I thought my twenty-five-pound weight loss would be the change most likely to be remarked about.

While the meeting point was technically the end of the route, we still had a few more miles to ride to get to the ocean. I said my goodbyes to Jeff and Kris, and slowly we all lined up in single file behind Joyce, who led us across the bridge. We did not care about traffic, evidenced by our riding in the middle of the lane. But no one honked. It was clear, with all of us sporting the same colorful Southern Tier shirt, that we were involved in an activity that provided us the privilege of owning the car lane.

After crossing the Bridge of Lions, we pedaled to Anastasia State Park. From there, it was a short ride to the edge of the dunes. Wally and I had a private moment as we rode together from the park entrance to the dunes. He told me how much he appreciated getting to know me, and I could tell he knew how much the ride meant to me. (I was saddened to hear that Wally passed away on January 25, 2020, from an unexpected heart attack. He was about to embark on another long-distance bike ride from San Diego through Mexico with Tom.)

We each walked our bikes about fifty yards from the edge of the dunes to the surf. It was not easy lugging Tank, weighing close to ninety pounds, through the sand. I had flashbacks to a similar experience in San Diego about nine weeks earlier. I remembered thinking at the time how I could not wait to repeat the same ceremonial dipping in Florida. And now it was over. No fanfare, just the personal satisfaction of knowing I had achieved something pretty cool.

The eight of us all stood close together, staring at the ocean, soaking in the moment. Everyone had their phone out, taking pictures of each other. Klaus asked a couple walking on the beach to take a group picture. The couple asked a few questions about our ride and then graciously snapped group pictures from each of our cell phones.

Half a dozen strangers were walking along the surf, out for an afternoon stroll in the cloudy, warm afternoon setting. I wondered if anyone had a clue that the eight cyclists on the beach had just completed a 3,100-mile cross-country ride. Probably not. Why would they? A few of the riders were in a rush to leave. We said our goodbyes and then walked our bikes back to the edge of the dunes. When everyone was back on the pavement, we decided to stage a short video of all of us riding together. It turned out to be comical because we could not figure out how to ride close enough without running into each other.

I rode my bike to the bike shop to have it shipped back home to New Jersey. Tom rented a car to transport him to his hometown of Virginia Beach. I got a ride from Tom to the Marriott next to Interstate 75, checked into my room, lay down on the bed, and wrote my last daily post on Facebook. I called Kelley and told her I could not wait to come home. My daughter, Jaclyn, posted on Facebook: "My dad's pretty damn cool!" (Well, Jaclyn, that is exactly how I feel about you, your sister Tara, and your brother Brian.)

I woke up early and hailed a taxi for the forty-five-minute ride to the Jacksonville Airport—the second time I'd ridden in a vehicle in two and a half months. At the airport, people were going about their daily business. I checked in and sat down at the gate to wait for my flight to leave. I was overcome with nostalgia for my nine weeks of crossing the United States, climbing mountains in the west, cycling through small towns in the east, until there were no more. I was excited to tackle the next phase of my life, but I was also apprehensive.

EPILOGUE

It was terrific to see Kelley at the airport in Newark, New Jersey, sixty-eight days after she dropped me off there in September. The feeling I had was familiar. The ride home felt like any other ride home after returning from a business trip. I was relaxed, knowing the days on the saddle were now a thing of the past. Kelley exited Interstate 287 in Morristown and then drove the last five miles on Route 24 to Mendham. My head turned from side to side—I was trying to ascertain if anything looked different from nine weeks ago. Nothing did. Kelley turned right onto our street and then left into our driveway. I was home. Trip over.

Later that day, I walked through town. One of my neighbors congratulated me on finishing the ride. That night, I met friends at the local pub, The Blackhorse Tavern & Pub. I had a blast reconnecting with family and friends. I loved talking about the ride, but I found it difficult to clearly and concisely communicate my experience. My mind raced as I spoke to friends.

Some people asked if I was going to write a book. My response was always an emphatic *no!* Writing was never something I'd been interested in doing. Plus, I questioned why anyone would want to read about my journey. Except for telling a handful of people, I didn't publicize the ride before I left. I did not raise money for a cause, primarily because I did not want to draw attention to myself. I rode across the country for *me*.

During the summer of 2019, I began to think differently. Instead of concluding that no one would want to read about my journey, I thought everyone should read about the fantastic experience I had cycling through small-town America, and I felt privileged to share it with others. On August 30, 2019, at our annual Mendham Labor Day Carnival, a friend, Jenny, helped push me over the edge. She told me, "Larry, your book is already written. Your daily Facebook posts."

The next morning, I began to write.

Occasionally, I am asked what it's like to ride a bike across the country. Simply put, it's cool but hard to explain. Imagine the anticipation of seeing a movie you have wanted to see for a long time. The advertisements increase your expectations and enthusiasm for seeing the show. On opening night, the theater is packed, and the show begins. For three hours, you are mesmerized, engrossed in the details unfolding before your eyes. There are twists and turns. The plot thickens. The story ends, the credits flow. Life goes on. Elevated expectations, a fantastic story, and then it is over. Riding coast to coast was an intense experience that, like a movie, had a finite beginning and end. Before and after the ride, my life was routine, but during the ride, I removed myself from the real world. I lived in a parallel universe, partially connected to family and partially connected to an unknown destination.

I always kept my eye on the prize and the big picture. There was never a second when I did not enjoy the journey. It's easy to meet new people when you walk into a convenience store or a motel wearing spandex bike shorts and a colorful but dirty cycling shirt covering a smelly, grungy body. The sound of clicking footsteps every time the metal shoe clip touches the floor and the presence of a fully loaded ninety-pound bike increases the level of curiosity of strangers. The natural reaction for most people is to engage in conversation. So many small towns make up the good ole United States of America. It is full of people living simple, wonderful lives. People that drive big trucks and motorcycles (no helmets), shop at Dollar General, and go to church—and there is a church on every corner, or so it seemed.

Eleven riders came together on September 15, 2018, in San Diego. We met each other, divided up the group gear, settled in for a good night of sleep, woke up, and started pedaling. We learned to compromise, support, and dig at each other. I enjoyed getting to know everyone. After celebrating the completion of our journey at the ocean, we shook hands, hugged, and returned to our everyday lives.

I decided to take this trip for several reasons. I wanted a physical and mental challenge that, if completed, would be rewarding, memorable, and different. I am glad I did it. I have no regrets! It would not have happened without Kelley's support and my kids (Tara, Jaclyn, and Brian) pushing me over the edge: "Dad, YOLO!"

I am forever mindful that I am susceptible to depression. Telling my story does lift a personal burden that I have carried for a long time. I could not wait to see my kids after arriving home from the airport. I'd taken hours of video and hundreds of pictures; there would be plenty of time to review after returning home. Standing on that beach in St. Augustine, everything seemed to blend. I was spent, tired, and ready to come home!

And for the record, I rode Every Frickin' Inch!!!

1984 Susquehanna University Sweet 16 Basketball Team

1985 C-Battery, 1-55 ADA, 5th Infantry Division,
Fort Polk, Louisiana Championship Basketball Team

1987 C-Battery, 2-61 ADA. 2nd Infantry Division,
Korea Championship Basketball Team

2004 Hoopaholics over 35 Basketball Team, Whidbey Island, Washington

2017 North Jersey over 50 Championship Basketball Team

1984 Soldiers in my platoon at Fort Polk, Louisiana

1988 Ranger School Graduation at Fort Benning, Georgia

*Army buddy Carlos on
6th Street Austin, Texas
on Oct. 21, 2018*

Larry, bike mechanic and Army buddy, John (r) at Austin bike shop on Oct. 22, 2018

*2016 The five Walsh Boys (Kevin, Tim, me, Dan and Dennis)
on vacation at the Outer Banks, North Carolina*

2016 Mom and Dad and the five Walsh Boys at the Outer Banks, North Carolina

2016 Mom and Dad

2017 Kelley and I celebrating our 25th wedding anniversary in Palm Beach, Florida

2018 The doting sisters, Tara and Jaclyn hugging their brother, Brian

*2019 My family (Tara, me, Kelley, Brian and Jaclyn)
in Morris Country, New Jersey*

Read on to get a first look at my next book,

FORTY TO FINISH

INTRODUCTION

May 30, 2019

I wore my green Columbia Silver Ridge Convertible hiking pants on United Flight #2415 to Portland, Oregon, the same ones I had donned eight months earlier for a United flight to San Diego when I began my three-month odyssey from self-doubt to self-confidence. A blue Smartwool 100 long-sleeve shirt and silver Northside Brille lightweight water shoes rounded out the ensemble, giving me an appearance that revealed my enthusiasm for the occasion.

The clothing easily fit into the Salsa Half-Frame Bike Pack, with adequate storage capacity to carry only essential items for my journey. Beginning on June 2, my Smartwool shirt would serve a much more critical purpose than casual travel attire: it would warm my torso as I cycled over five mountain ranges, including the Cascades and the Rocky Mountains, and into the heart of middle America.

The landing gear extended, the wing flaps opened, and the distinct roar attributable to the airplane's hydraulic motor signaled the final approach. A loud thump and screech of the brakes triggered an immediate roar due to the rush of high-speed air spewing out of engines. United #2415 touched down at 11:12 a.m.

I moved into the aisle and pulled a large mesh drawstring cinch sack carry-on from the upper bin. It carried all the clothing I needed for the next forty days. Roger, my travel partner and cycling mate, pulled his backpack from the upper bin.

Roger and I exited the terminal and walked directly to the taxi stand. "Hi! River City Bicycles on MLK Boulevard," I said to the driver. Roger and I gazed out the windows; Roger looked left and I stared right, numb to my surroundings on this late Thursday morning. During the twelve-mile ride from the Portland Airport to River City Bicycles on this sunny Portland day, we were mostly quiet.

I wondered, "Am I *nuts* to embark on a 4,200-mile bike race across America?"

Tank, the same Surly Disc Trucker touring bike I rode months before on the Southern Tier route, and Roger's recently bought All-City touring bike, appeared to be in great shape. Both had been rebuilt by mechanics at River City Bicycles after a long flight from New Jersey to Portland, Oregon, courtesy of BikeFlights. We browsed inside the bike shop located in Portland's Central Eastside district. Many shoppers filled the store. Portland must be a bike-friendly community, I thought, as I scanned the walls, floor, and tables full of cycling equipment and accessories. The volume of merchandise on display was greater than I had ever seen before. Portland's reputation as an environmentally friendly city entered my mind.

Two mechanics were working on bikes hoisted on repair stands behind the cash register. Roger and I were in no rush to leave the store; our bus from Portland to Astoria, Oregon, would not depart for several hours. I thought the one-hundred-dollar bike assembly fee was excessive, but we paid at the register and left the store. A large mural covering the concrete wall next to the store entrance grabbed my attention. I looked up and said to Roger, "How cool is that! Let's get a picture." The brightly multicolored abstract painting of an adult and a child facing the entrance created a focal point to attract attention—and perhaps more foot traffic.

I opened a Portland city map, located the bus station, and walked, instead of pedaling, toward the Greyhound bus station on NW 6th

Avenue near Old Town and Chinatown. I lugged Tank and my thirty-pound cinch sack across the Hawthorne Bridge over the Willamette River. Roger followed behind, single file. A slight haze blocked out the sun's intense golden rays, preventing them from penetrating directly onto us. However, the balmy early summer day created conditions in which I began to sweat before reaching the bridge.

My arms tired after a few minutes of pushing Tank from the left side. I switched to the right side, back to the left, then the right, then left, all the way to the bus station. We walked on Madison Street, turned north on Broadway, then right onto Burnside, zigzagging the last few hundred feet, and finally, after forty-five minutes, arrived at the bus station. The crowned tree branches and tall buildings of downtown Portland dominating the city streets protected us from the direct sunlight on Madison and Broadway, making the walk much more pleasant.

It had been many years since I'd visited Portland. I saw three homeless people sitting on the ground on Madison Street, leaning against a window. Each vagrant sat next to a cardboard sign; one read, "Poor and Hungry." I quickly looked away and continued walking without glancing at the second and third posters. Not because I didn't want to help, but because I didn't know if the man had a genuine need. His filthy, unshaven face and worn clothing caked with dirt gave the impression that he needed help. I did not know, though, so I chose to continue walking.

My mind flashed to a summer weekend in the late 1990s when my wife Kelley and I visited Portland during the annual Oregon Brewers Festival at the McCall Waterfront Park on the Willamette River. This event attracts dozens of breweries, food vendors, and musicians, transforming the park into an outdoor carnival. Hundreds roamed the area. Many wore tie-dyed clothing. Well before their time, tattoos were commonplace, and one memory stands out of a pregnant lady walking barefoot, abdomen exposed, full of tattoos from head to toe. Shortly after the turn of the century, Portland embraced its unique culture by calling itself America's Capital of Weird, borrowing the expression first started in Austin, Texas.[39] Portland's unique culture and way of life were on display then and again twenty years later; I was desensitized to seeing homeless people on the streets by my prior visits to the "Capital of Weird."

The bus station occupied the corner of a city block. A fence cordoned off a construction zone across the street from the station. Except for the occasional three- to four-second burst of clanging bell noise made by a powerful jackhammer, the area surrounding the bus station was still.

I walked inside the terminal and immediately thought of Grand Central in New York; there were high ceilings, a few people milling around. I felt unnoticeable in the cavernous room. I walked up to the ticket area, stood in line, and when it was my turn I asked, "Can you tell me if this is the right place to find the bus to Astoria?" adding, "I have a ticket for the 6:00 p.m. departure, and I'm also transporting a bike."

"Yes," the attendant said. "You can pick up the bus behind me on the side of the terminal. It usually arrives about thirty minutes before departure."

"Thank you," I said, and before walking outside to join Roger, I bought a Good Humor Giant Vanilla ice cream sandwich at a gift shop inside the terminal. I did not think consuming a 230-calorie ice cream sandwich mattered because, beginning June 2, I would start burning between seven thousand and ten thousand calories per day until I arrived at the Yorktown Victory Monument in Yorktown, Virginia.[40]

A man and woman exited the terminal walking next to their bicycles and joined Roger and me in a compact communal area next to the entrance.

"Hi, I'm Larry, and this is my buddy Roger," I said, while extending my arm to shake hands.

The man said, "I'm Garth" and the woman, "I'm Rylee," each taking turns to extend a warm greeting.

---

39 Theculturetrip.com
40 Caloriesburnedhq.com

"Are you two together?" I asked. They shook their heads in unison to signal it was their first time meeting each other.

Garth asked, "Are you guys here for the race?"

"Larry is, but I'm riding about a week and then returning home to New Jersey," Roger offered.

"I guess the both of you are in the race?" I continued.

"Yes" and "Yes," Rylee and Garth responded.

"Is this your first race? Do you have a goal?" I asked Garth.

He replied, "Yes, it's my first Trans Am. I want to finish in twenty-two days."

Rylee just shrugged when I asked her the same question, apparently not interested in divulging that information.

I calculated the math and concealed my marvel at the prospect of Garth cycling 190 miles per day for twenty-two straight days. Garth stood next to his bike, his left arm holding the bike frame and his right hand mimicking a finger gun by his side. He wore a bright yellow cycling shirt reminiscent of Tour De France jerseys covered with sponsorship and an orange reflective top, two prominent stripes over his shoulders and one around his waist. I focused my attention initially on his head and then on his arms and legs. A perfectly fitted curved helmet and glasses to protect from wind and sandblast, a smile that extended from ear to ear, and muscular and well-defined arms and legs conveyed that he was ready to go.

A few feet away, Rylee stood, both hands balancing her bike; a confident stance and an equally magical smile evinced her excitement and anticipation at tackling this epic journey. Roger leaned his bike against the Amtrak Rail Passenger Station and raised his right hand, pinky and thumb extended—a signal to relax and enjoy the moment. I snapped a photo, the first of many over the next forty days. Rylee and Garth soon disappeared; they presumably had a different game plan for traveling to Astoria.

At 5:30 p.m., the Greyhound bus arrived at the terminal. Roger and I got up from the bench we'd sat on for most of the afternoon and walked around the corner to the bus parking area. Passengers gathered and waited for the driver to give the signal to step up onto the bus. Surrounded by passersby, we loaded our bicycles into the bus's underbelly, destination Astoria, Oregon, point of departure for the Trans Am Bike Race (TABR). The sunny, sixty-five-degree afternoon had given way to a calm, crisp, fifty-degree dusk when the bus began traveling north on Highway 1.

I stared out the window in somewhat of a trance, gazing at the pine trees as the bus hummed along. I did not want to interact. I wanted to reflect, think, prepare.

Roger broke my concentration. "Larry, this is Michael. He's racing, traveling from Florida."

I smiled and introduced myself but quickly shifted my gaze to the outside world, contemplating and wondering. Happy to be present, but unclear what led me to this point.

Again, Roger broke my trance. "Larry, we'll be riding on this same road in a couple of days." I looked at the road and thought, *Yikes, it's a narrow shoulder to ride on.*

A few passengers disembarked at a bus stop in Seaside, the last before Astoria, which was seventeen miles further north. I dozed. The bus engine's rumbling white noise and darkness supplied the perfect sleeping conditions. The Greyhound turned onto Marine Drive and stopped in front of the Astoria bus stop drop-off point. At 9:00 p.m., I stepped down onto a dark, quiet street and scanned the surrounding area, looking in all directions. I felt at ease. A sense of calm came over me.

I wanted to be in Astoria, but I honestly did not comprehend the task ahead of me. We retrieved our bikes from the bus's underbelly and then began the short one-mile walk to the Commodore Hotel on 14th Street. Walking through town after dark, Roger and I had this sleepy town all to ourselves. On an otherwise dark street, blue neon lights and bright white bulbs lit up the hotel's front entrance. We glanced at a café attached to the hotel, relieved to know we had a place to get coffee in the morning. The Commodore, built in 1925, is a boutique hotel situated in the Downtown Historic District's heart.[41] It's small and intimate; when I entered, I felt like a personal guest in someone's private home rather than just a hotel occupant. The check-in desk was a mere opening in the lobby wall. Large metal room keys hung on a wall inside the open space. I could have reached in through the aperture and selected any room key I wanted. Instead, I rang the bell to summon the front desk attendant. The young woman welcomed Roger and me to Astoria and assigned us two rooms on the second floor. The first floor housed the front desk, the small lobby, and a walkway to the café entrance.

"Is there any place open in town to get a bite to eat?" I asked, expecting a different response than the one I got.

"The Fort George Brewery has really good burgers. Just up the road on Duane Street. Walk up 14th and you'll see it on the left," she shared before handing the large metal room keys to Roger and me.

The elevator and the room were small, barely large enough to fit Tank and me inside. The one communal bathroom and shower, down the hall and around the corner from my room, reminded me of a private house or bed-and-breakfast more than a modern hotel.

The TransAmerica Bicycle Trail began in 1973, during [our] co-founder's [Burden and Siple] ride from Alaska to Argentina, as nothing more than an ambitious idea for a way to celebrate the nation's upcoming 200th birthday. By June of 1976, the Trail was ready; the maps and guidebooks were published thanks to an enormous effort. Now cyclists were needed to ride it across the country. Given the name "Bikecentennial," organizers publicized the event, and thanks to strong word-of-mouth and its fortunate, prodigious publicity, 4,000 cyclists showed up for the ride.[42]

---

41 Commodoreastoria.com

42 www.adventurecycling.org

Most of the riders were in their twenties and had no experience with long-distance cycling. Hardly anyone wore helmets, and bikes were often of discount-store quality. The group set out to learn about themselves and America and have an experience of a lifetime.

In 2014, Nathan Jones, race founder and organizer, adopted the TransAmerica Bicycle Trail and created the Trans Am Bike Race (TABR). The original trail covers 4,200 miles, crossing ten states and five mountain ranges. It is one of the most challenging ultra-distance self-contained races globally. For many years I imaged riding my bike in the California desert and through the Imperial Sand Dunes. That experience was now behind me. Cycling over the Rockies was not something I had contemplated taking on so soon after returning home from my first cross-country ride in November of 2018. But now, I was fixated on cresting Hoosier Pass in the Rocky Mountains, cycling on endless Kansas roads, and looking up at that big Montana sky.

Nine months had passed since I had been employed. Finding a job was my priority when I returned home the day before Thanksgiving in 2018. Mentally, I was much better prepared to go about the task of discovering my next career opportunity. On one interview at the beginning of February 2019, I drove two hours to Princeton, New Jersey, in a snowstorm and sat through a three-member panel interview for a pharmaceutical sales manager job. I connected very well with the interviewers and thought I'd hit a home run. I did not get the job. I was disappointed but not discouraged. After reflecting on my responses to some questions, I realized I was more enthusiastic answering questions about the bike ride than about the job itself. Whether the interviewers noticed that as a signal to pass on me, I was unsure.

I continued to network with friends, browsing job sites, hoping to find something that would capture my imagination. But as days and weeks passed, I started to feign dedication to my job search.

While searching for a job, I also began sifting through pictures and videos I took on the Southern Tier cross-country ride. I knew my memory would fade over time, so I set out to complete a documentary before starting a new job. I wanted to memorialize the experience. I spent countless hours looking at pictures, videos, and extemporaneous notes from my fifty-seven days on the saddle the year before. I disconnected in my office, taught myself iMovie, and produced a video with music and subtitles. I set forth to tell my story of cycling from California to Florida. One Republic's song "I Lived," Fleetwood Mac's "Go Your Own Way," and Lee Greenwood's "God Bless the USA," plus other favorites, made for a perfect soundtrack to go with my journey from San Diego to St. Augustine, Florida.

I gave Kelley a sneak preview. "What do you think?" I asked.

She responded, "I love it. It's really good."

Kelley had been by my side for the past nine months and appreciated the positive impact the cross-country ride had on my mental well-being. She felt my story could help others coping with a similar situation— losing a job and dealing with feelings of depression. When she told me she loved the video, I knew I had a worthy goal to achieve. A dream that would challenge me to dig deep, discover my potential, and perhaps, in the process, help others.

Kelley and I invited friends to our home to watch the video on our Samsung sixty-five-inch TV screen. Kelley created a theatre experience by serving popcorn, soda, and a lot of candy. For Christmas 2018, my eldest daughter, Tara, had surprised me with a memory book that captured many of the pictures and descriptions I'd posted daily on Facebook the year before. Kelley placed the hardcover book on the coffee table in the TV room, hoping to inspire conversation. Our guests were engrossed, looking intently at the screen, periodically asking questions. I loved watching, reliving, and talking about my journey. When Lee Greenwood's "God Bless the USA" played and the credits rolled, friends teared up.

And something else happened. Memories filled my mind each time I watched. I started to think about riding across the country a second time. I had an inner restlessness and a longing for something more. The sense that something was missing created an internal tug-of-war, my brain whispering to me to find a job, my heart nudging me not to settle. I did not realize it at the time, but I still had the cycling itch.

I felt I could, and needed to, accomplish something bigger and more challenging than the Southern Tier. Cycling coast to coast, from the Pacific Ocean to the Atlantic Ocean, had brought me immense gratification. I'd answered a nagging question: was I physically and mentally capable of completing a cross-country bike ride? Overcoming significant obstacles such as extreme weather, loneliness, numbness in my extremities, and a sore butt only added to my feeling of satisfaction.

In March 2019, I watched a YouTube video of the 2016 TABR. Lael Wilcox overtook Steffan Streich on the last day of the 4,200-mile race, to win. She completed it in a little over eighteen days, the second-fastest time on record. Streich was leading with 130 miles to go. On the final morning, he started riding in the wrong direction, the effect of sleep deprivation. He realized his error when he met Wilcox in Bumpass, Virginia, cycling in the opposite direction. They rode together for a brief time, and Streich suggested they ride to the finish together. Reportedly, Wilcox responded, "This is a race," and sprinted the last 130 miles to become the first woman to win a major ultra-distance backpacking race, beating Streich by two hours.[43]

I pondered what it would feel like to race across America just like Lael did. Deep down, I yearned for the same feeling I'd had when I yelled, "I'm doing this!" in July 2018, when my heart won the tug-of-war and I committed myself to the Southern Tier Bike Tour.

Ken Simpson's compelling story of his experience in the 2016 TABR, revealed in an April 13, 2018, YouTube Ted Talk, also captured my imagination.[44]

I reflected for hours, sitting alone in my office. I yearned for the chance to once again pedal through small-town America connecting with strangers, anticipating the next surprise. But I also craved something

---

43 Gypsybytrade.wordpress.com
44 Ken Simpson Ted Talk (YouTube, April 13, 2018)

more. I wanted to experience complete solitude in the middle of America while pushing my physical limits. I put the Southern Tier ride in the rearview mirror and focused my full attention on competing in the 2019 TABR. The race began on June 2.

My inner restlessness and gnawing sense that something was missing disappeared. That same crisp thinking that was my North Star in 2018 had returned. I did not have much time. I needed to decide. The distance: 4,200 miles, crossing ten states and five mountain ranges. "Hell yeah! My name is written all over this race!" I thought.

Kelley supported my decision, but she hedged just a little. She asked, "How will you explain a second ride on a job interview?"

I did not have an exact answer. I replied, "I will figure it out." I had been out of work for close to a year. I rationalized the gap in employment. "What difference would a few more months make?" I thought. She convinced me that tackling the first ride would make me a more interesting person. As a fifty-six-year-old white male, it was a way to distinguish myself from others. I bought into her reasoning. But now, the roles were reversed. She was the one asking the question. Why?

There was only one explanation that made sense then and still does today.

And it is the lesson I want my children to remember: "Follow your passion, enjoy your life, and do not let others define you."

My three kids' reactions were different, a muted response this time. I sensed they were curious, wondering why Dad was doing this again.

Registering for the race was an ordeal. The TABR website was not accepting new entrants when I first inquired in late February. Contact information for the race organizer did not exist. I sent an email to a nondescript address I uncovered on the race website. I heard nothing. Precious days passed. Finally, after a couple of weeks, Nathan responded, telling me he had been traveling the country evaluating the impact that spring rainstorms had had on the Midwestern states' infrastructure. Flooding had caused the closure of many roads in Missouri, Kansas, and Illinois, three states on the TransAmerica Bike Trail.

In the first correspondence I received from Nathan on April 6, 2019, he asked why I wanted to race across America.

"So, you want to race the Trans Am Bike Race? A good question is, why? Why do you want to do this? Is this your calling in life? There are many other great events out there with a drastically lower risk for injury and death. For years, we have told people that there are no guarantees out on the open roads, and we have lost friends and family in the process. Continuing to run the race sometimes seems insurmountable, perhaps even foolish. We will continue, but we will evolve. People will continue to ask you why you do this. If you do not have an answer, we suggest you at least have an understanding and one that we wholeheartedly sympathize with."[45]

He signed off with "Cheers" and asked me to read the Racer Manual, complete the Stage 1 Application, and sign the waiver and the Racer Agreement. The unmistakable message was that TABR is not for the fainthearted, and I should consider other long-distance routes if I was not fully aware of the challenges, difficulties, and dangers associated with the race.

My email response was simple yet direct. "I want to test my physical and mental limits," I said, adding, "I recently completed the Southern Tier route." I knew what it took, both physically and mentally, to pull off a long bike ride, but now, I explained, I yearned for something bigger. I also highlighted my military experience and successful completion of the grueling two-month Ranger School. I thought it would not hurt to mention it and, if anything, might elevate my chances of hearing a positive response.

I was thrilled beyond belief when, on April 7, 2019, I received an email from Nathan, subject line "2019 Trans Am Bike Race Application Approved." I paid the nominal $290 entrance fee. (All race entrants are required to carry extreme sports insurance, obtain a medical clearance, and ride with a SPOT satellite tracking device.) I bought a Spot

---

45 Email from Nathan on April 6, 2019

Gen3 satellite tracking device rather than renting one from the race organization, an option for entrants who believed they could complete the race in thirty days or less.

I scoured YouTube videos in search of bike-packing ideas. Many racers carried all equipment in a single frame and seat post bag, limiting weight and air resistance. Lightweight titanium and carbon fiber bikes appeared to be favorites, designed with speed in mind. Anything that reduced drag was implemented, including helmets with curved and sloped surfaces to cut through the air. Many packed a bivvy, air mattress, bike tools, food, a navigation device, and minimal clothing to weather any significant rain or snow event.

I did not need, or want, to carry as much gear as I did on the Southern Tier ride. I split the difference but erred on the side of caution. On Tank, my chromoly steel Surly Disc Trucker bike, I carried my Big Agnes tent, sleeping bag, air mattress, multiple pairs of wool socks, two long-sleeve Smartwool shirts, two cycling shirts, three pairs of cycling shorts, Pearl Izumi long pants, riding shoes, and an extra tire. I placed personal identification, a pocketknife, a pocket light, a multi-tool, a waterproof note pad and pen, and pogey bait inside my handlebar bag. As much as I wanted to experience cycling through the Rockies, I did not want to be stranded at 11,000 feet in the Rocky Mountains riding through a snowstorm without the proper gear.

If the Southern Tier was my first ultra-distance ride without training wheels, the TABR was my Tour de France. I hunkered down. I needed to devise a plan. Where do I start? How do I begin to formulate a plan for a 4,200-mile bike race across the country? I would be on my own once the race started. There are no stages, rest days, help along the route. Every single decision is the responsibility of the racer, period.

The first step in formulating my plan involved performing a simple math exercise. I thought, "I completed the 3,100-mile Southern Tier in fifty-seven days, averaging fifty-five miles per day. Eighty miles was the highest one-day total. So, if I increased my average daily mileage total from fifty-five to eighty (which I believed was realistic), I would complete the 4,200-mile race in fifty-three or fifty-four days." Could I finish the 4,200-mile race in fewer days than it took to complete a 3,100-mile ride? "That would be pretty cool," I thought.

After returning home from my first ride, I had started to play pickup basketball again. Many of the guys I played with wondered where I had been the past few months. A few had heard about my ride from California to Florida, but most were unaware. Roger, a fellow hoopster and cycling enthusiast, intrigued by my journey, said he wished to take on a long-distance bike ride and considered joining me if I ever rode again. I piqued his interest. On Tuesday night, April 9, 2019, two days after Nathan approved my registration, inside the Mendham Township Middle School gymnasium, I told Roger I had entered the 2019 TABR. Within a week, Roger decided to join me on my trip to Portland—not to race, but to ride across the state of Oregon. He planned to take a week off from work and cycle hundreds of miles before returning home via Boise, Idaho. By mid-April, Roger and I were both committed and began to prepare in earnest. We hunkered down in a mad dash of effort, our departure to Portland about five weeks away.

In late April, Roger and I met at Simple Coffee in Mendham to review my bike-packing and riding plan. I wanted to bring Roger up to speed on the details of my plan as quickly as possible. Familiar people entered the shop to buy coffee and stopped briefly for casual conversations. Eyebrows were raised when friends learned of our plans to tackle such an epic journey. Looks of bewilderment and genuine fascination were conveyed through body language, often preceding, "Good luck, guys." I wondered if anyone we did not speak to in that shop had a clue that two middle-aged guys were concocting a plan for a bike ride across the country.

From mid-April to the middle of May, I increased training intensity. I lifted weights three or four times per week and rode a stationary bike between ninety minutes and two hours every other day. I varied my training routine; on days not on the stationary bike, I climbed Calais

Road, a twisty, winding, half-mile stretch of hill at a 15% grade, burning my legs to exhaustion on each climb.

From my hometown bicycle shop, Whippany Cycle in New Jersey, Chet offered to help me prepare for a grand ride once again. His recommendation to insert sealant inside the Schwalbe Marathon Plus Tires' inner tubes the year before had contributed to my being the only member of my tour group who did not experience a single flat tire the entire 3,100-mile journey. I hoped for a similar outcome on the TABR.

On Sunday, May 19, after attending my son's AAU basketball game, I took Tank to Whippany Cycle for shipment to River City Bicycles in downtown Portland, Oregon, courtesy of BikeFlights shipping service.

Kelley and I attended a live Styx concert on May 20 at the Mayo Performing Arts Center in Morristown, New Jersey. A throng of cheering fans packed the theater. With chin raised, chest out, and shoulders pulled back, I raised both arms above my head and clapped wildly when Styx started playing "Too much time on my hands," anticipating the familiar lyrics that had entertained crowds for decades. Like the lead singer, Tommy Shaw, who in the song contemplates his own experience of spending time in a bar in Michigan, I wondered if I too was spending too much time searching for something I would never find. But then "Come Sail Away" started playing. It was the one song that sent everyone immediately into a frenzy. Hundreds of cell phone lights appeared out of nowhere, everyone expressing their appreciation for the performance. The beginning lyrics touch on the nostalgia of the past, the ending verses a transition to follow your dreams by embarking on a journey into the unknown. An inner peace overwhelmed me, and I remember thinking I could not wait for the race to begin.

A family get-together at the Isle of Palms in South Carolina during Memorial Day weekend to celebrate my sister-in-law Gina's birthday was a fitting send-off, along with much raillery and kind gestures for a successful journey.

Early on the morning of May 30, Kelley drove Roger and me to the Newark airport. At the United terminal, I gave her a hug and a kiss. I remember thinking I would be thirty pounds lighter the next time I saw her. I stood in line at Gate 83, holding a cup of Starbucks coffee. I beamed, so happy to be on the road one more time. I was ready to go!

Forty to Finish coming soon!

ACKNOWLEDGMENTS

From late adolescence to authorship, my odyssey has been energizing, clear and clouded, sometimes perplexing, but always God's will. Writing this book was the last thing on my mind when my workday began on March 5, 2018, but I was blessed to be surrounded by incredible people—many of whom inspired me to think differently.

To my dad, who planted the seed.

To Jenny Rooney for pushing me over the edge by telling me, "Larry, your book is already written."

To Eric and Rosemary Carrera: thanks for introducing me to Kathy.

To Kathy Meis, Shilah LaCoe, and the entire Bublish team: thank you for guiding me through the process with patience, professionalism, and honesty, and for discerning that my story was worth telling, especially during these challenging times.

I am grateful to John, who helped me think critically about chronicling my tale. "You have two complete journeys," he said, "and I believe that they both deserve the attention of their own book."

Lindsay, editor and influencer, pulled me along with grace and wisdom from the first to the final draft. Thank you.

To all my friends who inspired me to keep writing when I had my doubts: thank you!

To Juliette Fredericks, who brought *Suit to Saddle* to life with a gripping, attention-grabbing cover: I am grateful for your efforts and for your sharing of your artistic talents.

To the four best bros, Tim, Dan, Dennis, and Kevin, for keeping each other young at heart, in spirit, and occasionally testing our competitive edge on the basketball court. We are fortunate to have Mom and Dad.

And to my loving children, Tara, Jaclyn, and Brian: there is nothing that gives me greater satisfaction than being your dad.

Finally, to Kelley—my wife, best friend, and confidant—your patience, perspective, love, and support during my difficult days helped me see the value in sharing my story, to pay it forward.

APPENDIX: BY THE NUMBERS

- Total distance – 3,120 miles
- Total climb – 88,892 feet
- Maximum speed – 38.95 mph
- Fastest 10-mile split – 24.42 mph
- Fastest full-day speed – 18.95 mph (55 miles from Marathon to Sanderson, Texas)
- Average distance per day – 55 miles
- Maximum day distance – 80 miles
- Maximum day climb – 5,115 feet
- Days away from home – 67
- Total riding days – 57
  - Sunny days – 36
  - Rainy days – 21
  - Nights camping under the stars – 39
- Towns ridden through – 229
- Hottest temperature – 106
- Coldest temperature – 35
- State borders crossed – 8
- Flat tires – 0
- People I met along the way – too many to count

CPSIA information can be obtained
at www.ICGtesting.com
Printed in the USA
BVHW041133140921
616733BV00014B/468